D1421438

"Steve Arterburn is the most qualified man I know to speak to the life transitions of men. I have seen him live out the principles of this book with my own eyes and sought, through imitation, to navigate my journey as a man in similar ways. He has never done me wrong as a man. Join me!"

—**Kenny Luck**, pastor and author

"Thanks, Steve and John, for telling us to take a minute, shut off the 'autopilot,' and think about how to live the second half. If more men would do what this book says, the midlife crises would change to midlife corrections and the second half could be much better than the first!"

—**Dr. Henry Cloud**, psychologist and author

"Finally there's help for men at that dangerous midlife crossroad in life. Steve Arterburn and John Shore outline for us how a man can make a smooth transition through midlife and avoid the midlife crisis that ruins so many men."

—**Dave Stoop**, PhD, psychologist and author

"Steve and I have shared many hours together laughing and sharing and reaching out to others. This midlife manual is full of great wisdom and will be a real help to men who want to soar through midlife rather than crash in a crisis."

—**Josh D. McDowell**, author and speaker

"The middle years can often be a bewildering and even disappointing time for men. However, it doesn't have to be that way. With Steve Arterburn's sound and clear guidance, these can be our best years. Steve combines years of experience in helping others with his own personal authenticity and a solid biblical base. You will be a better person for reading this book."

—**Dr. John Townsend**, psychologist, author, and speaker

FINDING SIGNIFICANCE
IN THE SECOND HALF

WORKBOOK

STEPHEN ARTERBURN

and JOHN SHORE | with ERIC STANFORD

MIDLIFE MANUAL FOR MEN

BETHANYHOUSE

MINNEAPOLIS, MINNESOTA

CONTENTS

INTRODUCTION

YOU COULD READ our book *Midlife Manual for Men* and in your head agree with the advice for middle-aged men to prepare for life's second half—but never apply that to yourself. In this workbook, though, we're going to turn the spotlight around and point it right at you. The central purpose is to help you personalize and individualize the message of *Midlife Manual for Men*. The workbook will enable you to make the message your own.

You're ready to take an honest look at yourself. You're committed to seeing who you might become in the second half of life, as God uses you. We honor you for this determination! And, friend, we're excited to think of all the wonderful adventures and challenges ahead of you.

Stick with it, and we promise you'll be changed for the better.

THE WORKBOOK AND ITS COMPANION PIECES

A warrior goes into battle not only with a loaded rifle but also with a helmet, body armor, and a communication headset. And maybe a pair of those cool night-vision goggles.

Likewise, *Midlife Manual for Men* does not stand alone. It comes accessorized with this workbook, DVD messages featuring me (Steve), and a leader's guide on CD-ROM that shows how to conduct a men's group on the topic. Our advice? Take advantage of it all.

We suggest that you read a chapter of the book and then go through the corresponding chapter in this workbook, on your own. A good schedule is to do this once per week until you're done—a period of seven weeks.

Meanwhile, we hope you'll also join a group studying *Midlife Manual for Men*. Or, if you don't know of such a group, maybe you could start one! If you combine attending a weekly men's group with reading the book, completing the workbook, and watching the DVD, you'll get the maximum benefit from the *Midlife Manual for Men* package.

The workbook, while correlating to the book's material, has several special features:

◆ Questions that will get you thinking about your own life

◆ Bible passages that teach God's perspective on the subjects most important to a man in midlife

◆ Profiles of biblical men whose lives illustrate the themes of each chapter

◆ Journaling spaces to help you record your thoughts for later recall or reflection

◆ "Prayer helps" to get you going or keep you going in your relationship with God

Work through this material faithfully and honestly. If you're married, share it with your wife. Most of all, make it a truly spiritual experience by opening your heart to what the Lord wants to show you about what he has in store for you as a midlife man of God.

MAN IN THE MIDDLE | 1

Your name:

Your age:

How you feel about being the age you are (check the box that comes closest):

☐ *I have serenely embraced my place in the chronological scheme of things and am actually looking forward to growing still older.*

☐ *It doesn't particularly bother me. Being middle-aged has its pluses as well as its minuses, and I intend to focus on the upside.*

☐ *Gee, thanks a lot for reminding me. I'm trying not to think about it!*

☐ *Get me out of here—I'm really twenty-two, aren't I?*

What do you hope to get out of this workbook?

From **Midlife Manual for Men**:

It happens to everyone fortunate enough to live long enough. Sooner or later we all experience that wake-up call that explodes like a bomb in the gut. BOOM!—and then you know it: You really are middle-aged. People having that moment tend to do a nanosecond evaluation of their life. And that's usually all it takes for them to realize that they wish they had done more, lived more, been more.

BOOM!

As the introduction to *Midlife Manual for Men* states, sooner or later we all get a wake-up call that tells us we're no longer young bucks. Our train has arrived at a station we never particularly desired to see: Middle Age.

Ben, forty-five, was in the marriage market again after a divorce. So when a pretty young woman standing in line at church to sign up for a singles group smiled at him, he straightened his shoulders, sucked in his gut, and smiled back.

Wow, he thought. *I wasn't sure about joining after all these years, but maybe it isn't going to be so bad after all. She's hot! And she actually seems like she's into me.*

"Hi," he said suavely to her. "Do I know you?"

"No," she replied, "but I feel like I know you. You look just like my dad."

Boom!

That's an amusing example. But there are many other ways a man can come face-to-face with his position in midlife. For example, how about when his father dies and he must face his new role as a member of his family's oldest surviving generation? Or what about the moment at his doctor's office when he realizes his body no longer seems indestructible?

What was your boom! *experience? That is, when and how did it really settle in that you had reached middle age?*

We don't know what Ben did when the hot young thing pushed him squarely back into the generation where he belonged. But we do know one of the first things most men do after the *boom!* is lowered: They start to look back on their life up to that date . . . with regret, with guilt, with wonder, with pleasure. This reflection is a good thing because it helps a man figure out how he got where he is.

What are your biggest regrets about how you lived the first half of your life? What gives you delight as you look back over your life so far?

Regrets

Delights

We'll say it again: reflecting on life's first half is good. Just don't get stuck there. Experiencing the *boom!* really is about figuring out what to do with the second half. And that's a process—whether you know it or not—you are going through with a whole lot of other men.

Welcome, brother!

> From **Midlife Manual for Men**:
>   Those of us who are actually in midlife are going through something that's truly unprecedented. Never in history have so many people at one time had to deal with what it really means to be, say, forty-five years old and know that you might very well still have half your life ahead of you.

YOU'RE NOT ALONE

The Baby Boom generation, as you know, created America's largest demographic boost ever. Most of us boomers are still around today, continuing the party. And so, as we point out in chapter 1 of *Midlife Manual for Men,* there are no fewer than thirty-nine million men going through midlife changes right now. That's a lot of company on the journey.

Furthermore, due to advances in longevity, the experience of being in life's middle is coming later for us than it did for earlier generations. If you, like Ben, have trouble remembering you're not a twenty-something dude anymore, there's a reason: Your age right now is "younger" in relation to one's presumed life span than it used to be.

> *Optional:* If you Google "life expectancy calculator," you should come up with more than one Web site that will let you enter parameters and then tell you how many more years of earthly life you can expect to enjoy. We can't vouch for the reliability of these tools, but you might find using them an interesting experience!

My remaining life expectancy:

How do you think your father and others of his generation experienced midlife the same way you are experiencing it? How did they experience midlife differently?

Who is someone around your age who is handling midlife poorly, and how? On the flip side, who is someone handling midlife well, and how?

What questions, concerns, or confusion do you have about living the middle portion of your life?

The fact that you can reasonably look forward to many more years means you've been handed a ticket to embark upon a new adventure. It's called midcourse correction. The first step is figuring out whether—and, if so, where—you've gotten off course.

From **Midlife Manual for Men**:

For the majority of guys, midlife is an experience to be ranked on a scale somewhere between "a cake walk" and a "trip to hell and back." In other words, chances are you are reading this book because you have a desire to take some stock of your life, recalculate your priorities, and position yourself to have a great "second half." Most of you are not in free fall, feeling like your entire world is coming apart—but maybe you do believe that certain pieces of it are indeed fraying at the ends.

MIDLIFE MISTAKES

Chapter 1 of *Midlife Manual,* on pages 24–32, identifies seven ways men can get off course in midlife. And that list is far from complete. In the book, review the descriptions of those seven "symptoms," then in the list below, check the ones you've fallen into.

If you've managed to invent another kind of midlife mistake, one different from the seven identified types, write it in the blank space at the bottom of the list.

If you haven't fallen into any of these things, then check one you think might place you most at risk, given what you've learned about your susceptibility to temptation.

(Check all that apply to you.)

☐ (1) Sustained depression

☐ (2) Restlessness

☐ (3) Acute irritability

☐ (4) Way too much "partying"

☐ (5) Endangering your finances

☐ (6) Becoming obsessed with sex

☐ (7) Having an affair

☐ (8) Other:

"Let us examine our ways and test them, and let us return to the Lord," advised a great prophet (Lamentations 3:40). In that spirit, skip down to each of the numbered sections below that corresponds to an item you checked in the list of midlife mistakes. There you will find suggestions about how to get back on course.

> From **Midlife Manual for Men**:
> The depression a man in midlife can suffer is often fueled by his conviction that he is chronically and profoundly underappreciated or underachieving, or only valued for what he achieves. It's truly a bad place to be.

(1) Sustained depression

Depression is not a mistake in the sense that you need to feel guilty for suffering from it. But it's definitely an indicator that somehow you've gotten off course.

What symptoms lead you to diagnose yourself as suffering from depression?

What (if anything) have you done to try dispersing depression's dark clouds? How has this worked for you?

In my counseling practice I (Steve) often see guys around my age try to "man up" and pull themselves out of depression through sheer determination. Does it work? Hardly.

But some combination of drug treatment and psychotherapy is successful for many sufferers—even for pig-headed men. If you think you have a sustained case of depression and not just a temporary bout with the blues, I urge you to speak with your physician and a mental health professional about putting together a treatment plan.

To the extent that your depression is due to problems in dealing with your stage of life, the *Midlife Manual for Men* should be another help in moving you beyond depression.

From **Midlife Manual for Men**:

All the regular, everyday stuff in your life now seems dull, each another indicator of a rut so deep and long it's as if you've awakened from a dream in which you were a huge, blind mole digging your way into your eventual grave. You want out, so you head straight up and bust through the ground and into the sun—enthralled by this bright new world and all the new people you've found in it, *great* people who have all these *great* new ideas, ways, and allurements! *Yippee!*

---

(2) Restlessness

A desire to throw out the old and plunge into the new can be one indicator that a man isn't handling middle age well. Is your enthusiasm for a new career, new technology, new music, new sports, new ideas, new friends, or anything else new a sign that you're trying to regain your lost youth?

How is your restlessness manifesting itself?

Now, don't get us wrong: Middle age certainly can be a prime time to start something new and renew one's enthusiasm for life. In a sense, that's what *Midlife Manual for Men* is about. But there's a right way and wrong way to go about it.

Step back and look at yourself. Why are you jumping into new things? If your motives are wrong or your approach is wrong, then piece your dignity back together and start thinking about where you really should be spending your time and energy.

> From **Midlife Manual for Men**:
> Persistent Middle-Age Fury is the kind that causes your wife to cry, your kids to storm out of the house, and your co-workers to say loudly enough for everyone to hear, "What's your problem, anyway?"

(3) Acute irritability

If you checked this box, we're sorry for the people you live and work with. But we're also sorry for you, because irritability is hardly more fun for the irritator than it is for the irritatee. (Hmmm, is *irritatee* a word?)

How have you been irritable with others? Give specific examples.

What do you think is driving that irritability?

Willpower alone won't cure irritability. You have to go to the root of the problem. That's why we hope you'll stick with *Midlife Manual for Men* to the end, since redirecting your life's course should clear up some of the irritability.

But in the meantime it's helpful to become more aware of how you have been treating others badly. And you can try to behave better with your loved ones, can't you? Oh, and apologize for how you've been acting.

> From **Midlife Manual for Men**:
> Most men don't struggle with substance abuse. But it can be a temptation for a man who has been knocked far enough off his bearings that he is, in this way, driven to get even *more* lost than he already is.

(4) Way too much "partying"

You might think that our generation—famous for "turning on, tuning in, and dropping out"—might have finally reached the point of just saying no to drugs and alcohol. Oh yeah? Studies show that among boomers, drug use (especially marijuana) actually is up in recent years. And of course we do our share of overindulging in alcohol.

We have news for you: Acting like a college student by playing with mood-altering substances won't make you twenty-one again. And your middle-aged body is less capable of dealing with that sort of abuse than ever before.

What are the signs that you party too hardy?

If this area is a problem for you, consider getting professional help to stop. Find other ways to deal with who you are as a man in midlife.

After the high, you'll always drop back to real life. Make it a *better* real life.

> From **Midlife Manual for Men**:
> For some of us, there's something about the pressing of midlife that can really make a guy want to buy all kinds of things that he wouldn't dare to if being middle-aged hadn't caused him to go a little (or a lot) nuts.

(5) Endangering your finances

Sure, splurge a bit on yourself now and then. You've earned it. (Haven't you?) But you still have responsibilities to yourself and your family to manage money wisely. And the *pop* you get from having new toys isn't going to last long or fundamentally change who you are.

What have you bought that you didn't really need or couldn't really afford?

If you've been spending money to make yourself feel young again, you may need to wake up to what you've been doing and get back on a course of financial prudence. On the other hand, if you've gotten yourself or your family into real trouble with debt, look into professional financial counseling.

> From **Midlife Manual for Men**:
> A guy feels his life is half over, and then BOOM!—he does the unthinkable: He commits the worst of the worst sin, and he has no idea that it was compensation behavior, that he was only trying to prove he still had it. And in the wake of acting out come broken dreams and heartaches.

(6) Becoming obsessed with sex

In this world of ours it's getting harder and harder to avoid lust triggers—suggestive images in ads, sexy plots in shows and movies, revealing clothing styles, and so on. We might even be pulling the trigger ourselves by going to porn. Our fantasies run wild. An affair may be only a step away. If that.

A few years down the road our libidos might shrink to a point where sexual temptation doesn't seem to affect us. But in middle age we haven't reached that point yet. (That's nice, in a way, of course!) And so we have to be vigilant and not use our sexual desires to compensate for our loss of youth.

How have you lost discipline regarding sexual purity?

What has your impurity cost you and others?

I (Steve) have written a whole other book about battling sexual temptation. Read *Every Man's Battle* (WaterBrook Press) if you need help with living in purity.

From **Midlife Manual for Men**:

[Having an affair] is where the fantasies very often rooted and nurtured in the hothouse of Midlife Imaginations blossom forth into the ultimate Flytrap *a la* Venus (or another word that, um, rhymes with Venus). Verily, this is the mother of all midlife crisis symptoms.

---

(7) Having an affair

We like to joke around even when discussing some pretty serious topics; it keeps things lighter and more manageable. But this is one midlife mistake we can't joke about.

What role (if any) did your struggle with aging play in your infidelity?

Reread the section in chapter 1 called "Having an Affair," pages 29–32, and especially note the action steps we recommend for moving past an affair.

What are you prepared to do today to start recovering from infidelity?

Don't wait to act. An affair can lead to unbelievably painful consequences. It's always been that way and always will be.

A BIBLICAL MAN IN THE MIDDLE: DAVID

We men who have lived through the cultural revolution of the 1960s, the malaise and decadence (not to mention the embarrassing clothes and hairstyles) of the 1970s, the conservative resurgence and yuppie greed of the 1980s, the dotcom boom of the 1990s, and on into the terrorist-threatened twenty-first century may think we invented the midlife crisis. But we did not. We've just added our personal style to it. In reality, men throughout history have had to deal with the what-do-I-do-now question of midlife—and they haven't always dealt with it very well.

Once upon a time a national leader noticed an attractive and cooperative young woman who made him feel sexually potent again, and in a moment of gonad-fired irrationality he decided to take advantage of the situation. No, this is not Bill Clinton and Monica Lewinsky. We're talking biblical history here: David and Bathsheba.

You know the story, right? Well, even if you think you know it well, reread it anyway and refresh your memory. Get your Bible and check out 2 Samuel 11 to see the kind of mistake a successful man in midlife got himself into when he was feeling restless and randy. Do it now; we'll wait. *Tick tock, tick tock . . .*

Back already? Okay, with your Bible still open in front of you, answer these questions:

What decision did David make that led to his having time on his hands when he normally would not have? (See verse 1.)

How might idleness or self-indulgence lead you to handle your middle-of-life experience in a less than godly way?

Imagine David pacing the flat roof of his palace one evening, then looking down and seeing another man's pretty young wife sponging her limbs. What kind of thought process do you think might have gone through his head as he decided to take a bath in sin with Bathsheba? (See verses 2–4.)

What is the voice of temptation whispering to you about how you should react to where you are in life right now?

How did David dig himself deeper into sin while trying to climb out of the situation he'd created? (See the rest of 2 Samuel 11.)

What sort of a mess could you get yourself into if you obeyed the voice of temptation in your own life?

To learn the consequences of David's midlife mess-up, read 2 Samuel 12. It fell out like this: David (to his credit) felt real guilt and went through real repentance when confronted with his wrongdoing. But that didn't stop God from letting him experience the consequences of what he had done.

◆ "The sword [would] never depart from [his] house" (2 Samuel 12:10), that is, his family would be plagued with violence for the rest of his life.

◆ Someone close to him (his son Absalom) would sleep with his wives—in public no less.

◆ The son he and Bathsheba had conceived in adultery would die.

All this came to pass. And though David lived a full lifetime and remained king, the second half of his life just didn't have the first-half sparkle. He no longer had the golden touch that had made amazing things happen. He struggled with his loved ones and remained ensnared in plots, counterplots, and all manner of violence.

Poor David. He faltered in faith during his midlife crisis, and he lived to regret it for the rest of his life.

What lesson(s) does the example of David hold for you as a man in the middle of life?

RECALCULATING THE ROUTE

Wouldn't it have been great if David had gotten his life on track before he looked down at a soapy Bathsheba? Wouldn't it be great if you set a new course *before* you headed any farther down a dead-end path?

Just as a car's GPS device calls out "recalculating route" when you get off course, so you can reposition yourself in life. As a matter of fact, you can make your second half better than your first. Bonnie Prudden says, "You can't turn back the clock, but you *can* wind it up again."

I (Steve) didn't have any choice when it came to recalculating my life route. An unexpected divorce when I was forty-six forced me to rethink my identity and my future.

I pray you won't have quite so violent a push into recalculating. But recalculate, you must. Given your current age, think about what you can do to make the most of the one life God has given you.

Life is short, and it's getting shorter all the time. *Now* is the time to make adjustments.

As of right now, what is it in your life that you would like to recalculate?

We'll help you much more with recalculating as we go through the rest of this workbook together. But for now, let us point something out.

When we talk about recalculating, we're not talking primarily about accomplishing more. It's not about starting a business or buying a second home. Nor is it about the kinds of things people often put on their "things to do before I die" lists. Sure, it might be great to see the Taj Mahal. But we're talking about something much more important.

Recalculating your route as a Christian man in midlife means *becoming more familiar with what God wants of you and then going about it*. This is spiritual more than practical. Who knows? It might include starting a new business or visiting India, but its goal is doing God's will.

This is why we pray that this workbook will be part of a life-changing *spiritual* process for you. More important than filling in every blank or answering every question is spending time every day praying and listening to God—basically, being in touch with your Creator.

If we're open to God, he will tell us where he wants us to go next. So let's pray daily with David, that biblical man in the middle:

Search me, O God, and know my heart;
 test me and know my anxious thoughts.
See if there is any offensive way in me,
 and lead me in the way everlasting.
 (Psalm 139:23–24)

Your life's second half might last a few decades. But eternity is never-ending. Prepare for an eternity with God by following him boldly throughout your remaining years here on earth.

How will you incorporate into your schedule speaking to and listening to God?

It's wonderful to be with you on this journey, brother! And we hope you'll travel with other men by joining a group studying *Midlife Manual for Men*. Have courage and go with God.

Prayer

Well, God, here I am. If you choose to grant me a full number of years, then I'm standing right in the middle of the life you've given me. What is it you want to make of me now? Anything you want for me—that's what I want.

Show me the wrongdoing and the rightdoing of my past. And show me how you can build on that past to take me somewhere great in your sight. Show me your highest will for my second half of life, and mold my will to yours.

As I read and write and think and pray and talk about being a man in midlife, guide my steps onto the course where I belong today. Make me a man after your own heart, worthy of hearing your "Well done."

Amen.

Journey With God Journal

*Things I feel God is saying to me about recalculating
my course for the second half of life:*

Notes for My Men's Group

*Things I want to be sure to bring up at our first session
of studying* Midlife Manual for Men *together:*

25

Notes on the DVD

Things I want to remember from Steve's message in scene 1:

HE-MAN OF THE UNIVERSE | 2

IN THE FILM *The Right Stuff,* America's greatest test pilot, Chuck Yeager, regretting his decision to pass up the chance to become an astronaut, commandeers an experimental jet, flies it so high that he can see stars glimmering through the upper atmosphere, and then plummets toward earth after the jet stalls out. Fighting to maintain consciousness, Yeager ejects; then, tumbling through the air, he struggles with his parachute, trying to get it to open.

After the landing, an ambulance containing a medic and Yeager's friend Ridley heads for the crash site. Meanwhile, Yeager, his face blackened and bloody, strides out of the desert with a tower of smoke rising in the background.

The medic says to Ridley, "Sir, over there. Is that a man?"

Ridley says, "Yeah, you're d—n right it is."

Yeager was a *man,* all right. A he-man, you might even say.

Movies do a great job of showing us he-men in action.

What's *your* favorite tough-guy movie? Maybe it's newer, such as a Jason Bourne film, where Matt Damon chops six foes into senselessness and then uses a subcompact car to outrun the entire police force of Prague—all before breakfast. Maybe

27

it's older, a classic like *The Searchers,* in which John Wayne's character spends years on horseback tracking down one little girl snatched by Indians, then is such a loner that he can't even enter a house to celebrate his achievement.

These kinds of films speak to something deep inside us men, don't they?

Your favorite tough-guy movie:

How important is it for you to be able to see yourself as a tough guy? Why do you think that is?

We're all in favor of men being masculine. But as we point out in chapter 2 of *Midlife Manual for Men,* we worry sometimes that masculinity has become so misrepresented in our society that we men can become frustrated and frustrating tyrants instead of the godly servant-leaders we're meant to be.

The good news, as we see it, is that middle age is a time when we can begin to live out a masculinity that's seasoned by experience and surrendered to God. After all, he's the only real He-Man of the Universe. The rest of us would-bes are his creatures who have been made in the masculine form of his image.

To become the kind of men God wants us to be, we must start peeling off the layers of false masculinity that the world and our own foolishness have overlaid on us.

SO-CALLED MEN OF STEEL

So far, in the course of your life, what have you said good riddance to? Diapers? Teenage acne? Your first junker car? Your college loans? A boss who graduated from the Vito Corleone School of Management?

Likewise, there may be things in your view of manhood you need to say good-bye to.

From **Midlife Manual for Men**:

For most of us, the bottom line on being a guy—a boy, a teenage boy, a young man, a man, a middle-aged man, an old man—is that it's almost always about . . . *machismo*. Being a Man's Man, strong and stoic. That is what we are, what we do. Or at least that's what most of us feel like we're supposed to be.

He-Man Good Riddance #1: The terrible burden of unceasing expectation that comes with being He-Man of the Universe

If we buy into the idea that every guy should be a He-Man, a Superman, we're under heavy pressure to give a tip-top performance every time. When it comes down to it, we're just regular guys. We've got our flaws, our limitations. Sometimes we're going to fail.

It's better not to pretend we're more than we are.

Describe one time when, out of masculine pride, you pretended to know more or to be stronger or tougher or more capable than you really were.

For you, what will it mean to stop trying to act like Superman and just be who you are?

> From **Midlife Manual for Men**:
>   We may not, as in times gone by, rule via big clubs and heavy rocks we toss with alarming accuracy, but the fact remains that on the food chain that is life, men *are* the big dogs. Whether we sense it or not, though, this power often fuels an undue sense of entitlement.

He-Man Good Riddance #2: Our enduring, ultimately crippling sense of entitlement

In many ways it's a man's world. And the power we have just by virtue of being men can go to our heads. If we let ourselves, we can start throwing our weight around and become obnoxious jerks.

The proper response to this error is to recognize the power we hold and start using it responsibly.

Do you agree or disagree with the notion that men have an advantage in our society? Why?

If you were to ask your most loving critic (say, your wife) how you reveal a sense of entitlement, what do you think this person would say?

> From **Midlife Manual for Men**:
>   Deep down inside, all of our iconic Strong and Silent types are full-on emotional basket cases. The reason they barely ever talk isn't because they're so perpetually cool and collected. They don't talk because they know if they do they'll start crying and whining in utterly career-destroying or image-breaking fashion.

He-Man Good Riddance #3: Suppressing our emotions

The popular notion is that men are not supposed to feel. Or rather when we start to feel, we're to stuff the emotions deep down inside so we can remain free to act in the world around us.

But as a counselor, I (Steve) have seen over and over again how a man's repeated suppression of emotions masks turmoil inside. It also limits his abilities to relate well to God and to the important people in his life. A real man lets himself feel his feelings.

Which description below best describes where you fall on the spectrum as a "feeler"? (Check one.)

☐ Emotions? What emotions?

☐ I don't show it much on the outside, but the big things in life do affect me.

☐ I'm still a man's man, yet women rightly find me to be "sensitive."

☐ I let it all hang out all the time.

Do you feel a need to open yourself up more to your own emotions? Why or why not? If so, how could you go about this?

From **Midlife Manual for Men**:
    When it comes to handling an intense personal issue, Plan A for most guys is Clam Up and Isolate. We men don't in general take pleasure from the company of others when we're trying to work out something that's very seriously just about us.

He-Man Good Riddance #4: Going it alone

When trouble comes, the Guy Way is for a man to say nothing, go off by himself, and deal with it alone. Effective? Usually not.

We need to remember that God's Way is for us to live in community, not as Marlboro Man loners. We need to develop the ability to work through our problems with our wives or with others close to us.

Think of a tough time you've been through. What was it? How did you deal with it? How effective was your approach?

How could you open up to others more the next time you're struggling?

REAL MEN

Before we start giving in to the we-should-feel-guilty-just-because-we're-men attitude that seems to float around rather freely these days, let's turn from what we should say good riddance to and instead look at what we should say howdy to. After all, there are a lot of good things about being men, especially about being men in midlife.

From ***Midlife Manual for Men***:
From a young age, men are socially inculcated in the Ways of Power. Knights slaying dragons and rescuing princesses; cops going after bad guys; firemen rushing into burning buildings; soldiers sacrificing themselves for the common good . . . we guys grow up surrounded by and acutely sensitive to endless examples of what amounts to the Proper Care and Feeding of Power.

He-Man Pure Gold #1: Your understanding of the nature of power

Power has a way of corrupting those who wield it. And power misused can become one of the world's most destructive forces. But none of this means that power necessarily is bad in itself. Sometimes power needs to be wielded, and those who wield it righteously are worthy of honor. This includes us as men.

What is an example of how you are powerful?

From **Midlife Manual for Men**:

By middle age we (usually) have earned the right to claim real clarity on the issue of responsibility. We know what it means, what it costs, what it entails. We know how careful we should be before committing to anything more substantive than declaring the correct time to someone on the street. We understand our actions and our promises have (usually very predictable) consequences.

He-Man Pure Gold #2: Your true understanding of, and comfort with, responsibility

No one naturally likes being responsible. But over time we learn what our selfish irresponsibility costs us and others. We're willing to do the right thing and fulfill our duty . . . time after time.

In what ways can the people closest to you (wife, kids, friends, co-workers, and so on) count on you to do what you're supposed to do?

> From **Midlife Manual for Men**:
> Our job, as thoughtful, wanting-to-be-wise middle-aged guys, is to as much as possible make our nature like God's. And of all things, God is *the* king of Slowly but Surely.

He-Man Pure Gold #3: Your understanding of how, little by little, mountains can be moved

Young guys are impatient. By middle age, we're more likely to realize that persistence and determination can achieve results that restless energy never could.

Does our sticking in there and plodding along mean we've become boring? Well, maybe so, at least from a certain perspective. But in the fable of the tortoise and the hare, the tortoise wins the race—and we want to win whatever race we're in. *That's* not boring.

Do you find that you're becoming more patient and persistent than you used to be? If so, what benefits have you received as a result?

> From **Midlife Manual for Men**:
> We get out there and do stuff. We try stuff. We risk stuff. We look at what's there, and if we think it needs to be rearranged, we put our You Know What on the line and start messing with that thing. We see what happens!

He-Man Pure Gold #4: Your legitimate claim to bravery, born of almost countless challenges faced and overcome

Bravery isn't always about the kind of heroics we see in war movies. It's not always the sword-in-hand daring we read about in fantasy stories. Bravery is also what characterizes a man when he overcomes challenges as a husband, father, and provider and in every other role he lives out before God and humanity. Indeed, day-to-day bravery is sometimes the noblest kind of all.

Are you brave? How do you know it?

Speaking of *brave*, there's someone we want you to meet.

A BIBLICAL HE-MAN OF THE UNIVERSE: SAMSON

If ever there was a He-Man in Bible times, it had to be Samson. Don't you agree? His story is told in Judges (chapters 13–16) because he was a "judge" (tribal boss) back in the days before Israel had a king.

Here was a guy who spent much of his life behind enemy lines, an Israelite living among Philistines. Today that would be like . . . well, like an Israeli general living in the Gaza Strip (which geographically corresponds to Philistia of old). Apparently things don't change that much. Sigh.

Anyway, Samson seemed to court danger by hanging out among Philistines who wanted him dead, robbed, and humiliated, not necessarily in that order. But his boldness and incredible strength were such that he wasn't afraid to challenge them—and to mess with their heads in the process. Plus, he had a thing for Philistine girls.

Remember those Charles Atlas ads in the back of the comic books you read as a boy, the guy's muscles bulging above leopard-pattern shorts? Samson would have made Chuck look like a weenie. Don't believe it? We've got the proof.

Evidence #1: One time Samson posed a riddle to thirty Philistine guys, and he was so sure they'd never figure it out that he offered them each a suit of clothes from Brooks Brothers (or the era's equivalent). In turn, they threatened Samson's Philistine wife so that she nagged him for a week to get the answer, which she then passed on to them. When they knew the right answer, Samson knew what had happened. He made good on his promise by slaughtering thirty Philistines and taking *their* Brooks Brothers suits.

Evidence #2: A little later, when Samson was away from Philistia on a trip back home, his father-in-law gave Samson's wife to another man. Finding this out, Samson was really mad—something you didn't want to see if you were of the Philistine persuasion. This time Samson caught three hundred foxes (in itself, quite a feat), tied them tail to tail in pairs with a torch attached to each pair (another feat), and set them loose in the Philistine fields to burn up the crops. Interesting strategy.

Evidence #3: When some of the Philistines murdered Samson's wife and her father, Samson pulled out all the stops. He picked up the jawbone of a donkey (wouldn't be our first choice for a weapon, but whatever) and killed *one thousand* Philistine men with it. Suddenly the Bourne movies seem more believable, huh?

Samson. A He-Man, we're telling you. But you know there must be a "rest of the story," and there is. Samson finally lost his supernatural strength. You see, Samson had been dedicated as a Nazarite from birth, and one of the special Nazarite characteristics was that they were not to cut their hair. So Samson had Fabio hair to go with his Charles Atlas pecs. In his case, if his hair were cut, his strength would be cut off along with it.

We've summarized the story enough. Get your Bible and read some of it for yourself: Start with Judges 16:1–22.

Who or what did Samson have to blame for his loss of strength? Why?

Now check out Judges 16:23–31.

Who or what did Samson have to credit for his final return of strength? Why?

Complete this sentence: A lesson I take away for myself from the Samson story is:

Samson had spectacular powers, divinely given to him, but they were mostly wasted when he hung out with God's enemies and dallied with women he had no right to. Yet in the end, when he was blind, he learned to see. He turned to God. He found integrity at last.

From **Midlife Manual for Men**:

Within you is the strength and wisdom to let go of the worldly things and steadfastly adhere to the magnificent things: Your God. Your knowledge of what's right and wrong. The people you love. The commitments you make. The promises you extend. The moral structure you determine is worthy of your fidelity. The integrity to which you have a rightful claim.

STICKING WITH WHAT'S RIGHT

In the classic movie *To Kill a Mockingbird,* small-town Alabama lawyer Atticus Finch (played by Gregory Peck) defends a black man named Tom Robinson, who has been falsely accused of raping a white woman. The conclusion to the trial is foregone. A white jury in this racially biased community during the Depression can be trusted to convict any black defendant without regard to the evidence.

Many of the townspeople try to get Finch to pull out of the trial, but he refuses. Perhaps more painful, he learns that his kids, Scout and Jem, have been subjected to abuse by other children because of what their father is doing. He even faces down a mob bent on lynching Robinson. Finch believes in serving the ends of justice, even when doing so challenges long-held assumptions and puts him and his family at risk.

Along the way, Finch—the kind of dad we all wish we'd had—helps Scout and Jem learn a similar lesson about accepting a strange neighbor named Boo Radley, whom many consider to be insane. "You never know someone," Atticus tells Scout, "until you step inside their skin and walk around a little."

In case you haven't seen the film, we won't say how the trial or the relationship with Boo turns out. Suffice it to say that in his courtly southern way, Atticus Finch shows us what it's like to stick to principles no matter what. He's a man of integrity.

Integrity is steadfast adherence to moral or ethical principles. More particularly, for Christians, integrity is steadfast adherence to God's way of doing things as revealed in the Bible. That can be a pretty tall order for flawed, not-so-he-mannish men like us.

Life is complex. Decisions aren't easy. The right course isn't always plainly seen. It takes determination to hold to God's standard in this world, and it takes accumulated wisdom to know how to apply that standard in our complex lives. This is what a man in midlife can be equipped to do as he opens his spirit to the guidance of God's Holy Spirit.

What are some areas of your life where you are called to act with integrity?

How "integritous" have you been lately?

What will help you grow as a man of integrity?

The apostle Paul wrote, "As for you, brothers, never tire of doing what is right" (2 Thessalonians 3:13). We couldn't say it any better.

A HE-MAN'S THINGS TO DO

Check out the "Things to Do" section of chapter 2, on pages 69–71, in *Midlife Manual for Men*. Then enter your responses below.

(1) Sources of ideas about manliness

When you were growing up, what qualities were you taught (either in so many words or by example) that a man should have?

How have these ideas about manliness hurt you? Helped you?

To what extent should you embrace them? Replace them?

(2) Models of manhood

List three men whom you have known personally and also admire.

(1)

(2)

(3)

What qualities do you admire about each?

(1)

(2)

(3)

How do these qualities match up with the qualities our culture tells us Real Men ought to possess? How do they fail to match up?

(3) Advantages of being a man

How does being a man help you in life?

How are you taking advantage of your privileged status in this "man's world"?

(4) Disadvantages of being a man

How is being a man not such a great thing?

Do you ever wish you were a woman or a kid instead of a man? Why or why not?

(5) Relationship with God

What typically masculine qualities have interfered in your relationship with God?

What do you feel God is saying to you about these qualities in your life?

(6) Changing a source of stress

What is something (or someone) in your life that causes you stress?

Qualities this stressor possesses	Qualities you wish it (or they) would possess

How (if at all) can you change this thing/person to be more like what you'd want it/them to be?

If you can't change it/them, how can you learn to live with it/them?

Prayer

Lord, do you sometimes laugh at my pretensions to super-manliness? I'll bet you do. I'm going to try to laugh too and not take myself so seriously.

I don't want to be some kind of pumped-up, faked-up He-Man. But I do want to be a real man, with all the honor and nobility belonging to that role. So I'm asking you to help me purify my notions of manhood and become the man you want me to be. That will be more than enough for me.

You're the He-Man of the Universe! You and only you, Almighty God! I worship you and am in awe of your absolute power and unstoppable will.

Amen.

Journey With God Journal

Things I feel God is speaking to me about being a real man made in his image:

Notes for My Men's Group

Things I want to be sure to bring up at our second group session:

Notes on the DVD

Things I want to remember from Steve's message in scene 2:

SON 3

WE DON'T KNOW what kind of parents you had. Maybe you were lucky and had a *Leave It to Beaver* childhood, your father dispensing wise advice while your mother baked cookies, wearing her pearl necklace. Gee, Wally, that's really neat. But on the other hand, maybe your parents resembled Homer and Marge Simpson. *Doh!*

The Beav or The Bartman. Whatever your early years were like, we're pretty sure about this: You have some great memories and also some hurts that haven't entirely gone away. This chapter is a chance for you to process some of that stuff and then go on with a healthier legacy from your childhood for the second half of life.

To start, write down words that come to mind when you think about your dad and your mom (*loving, never around, funny, distant*, whatever). Don't think about it too much, just throw down some words. This will give you a baseline for your attitude and you can go on from there.

Dad   Mom

As you prepare to step back in time to review memories, go to your heavenly Father in prayer, asking him to give you his perspective on your childhood and show you what you can learn from it.

> From **Midlife Manual for Men**:
> The way it is supposed to work is that when we show up, looking like miniature Fred Mertzes (of *I Love Lucy* fame) and screaming our lungs out, we're about as helpless as helpless gets—and we stay helpless for a long time. Thoughtless burp machines though we may seem to be, we are collecting and processing massive amounts of information about who we are and what we're supposed to do and be. And we acquire and absorb most of that knowledge from Mom and Dad.

HOW NICE TO BE GROWN UP

Even if you had a good boyhood—and we hope you did—there are still some things we're sure you're glad to be rid of. And we're not talking about fear of "girl cooties," or about the lime green leisure suit you wore in the seventies.

If sometimes you're not so crazy about being middle-aged, think about these things you've happily outgrown.

> From **Midlife Manual for Men**:
> When you're a kid, what choice do you have in . . . well, any matter at all? As a baby, if you want to go somewhere, you have to wait for someone to *carry* you there. Terrible! And if you get hungry, there's no way you can just order in a pizza. Instead, you just have to hope someone notices you're hungry and feeds you. Again, less than ideal.

Son Good Riddance #1: Being physically dependent

Some animals are independent practically from the time they are dropped from the womb or punch their way through an eggshell. Not so the human "creature." Starting with the time you were carried around in others' arms, fed from a breast, and had your little fanny pinned into a diaper, you were heavily dependent on bigger people, particularly Mom and Dad. Becoming capable of feeding, clothing, cleaning, transporting, and entertaining yourself was a process taking *years*.

How nice to be done with all that physical dependence!

What kind of physical independence can you remember being thrilled to undertake, sometime in childhood?

From **Midlife Manual for Men**:

The idea that because you're a kid nothing you think is valid is one of the worst things about childhood. While it's never really been clear why it should be assumed that a taller, hairier human is necessarily smarter than a shorter, smoother one, this prejudice persists.

Son Good Riddance #2: The assumption that your knowledge and/or understanding is insufficient

For some reason, grown-ups believe they have to think for kids. Now, obviously grown-ups do know more than kids and have had more experience. But if you're a kid, it can be enormously frustrating when adults don't even listen to your perspective on things. Sometimes kids "get it" better than adults.

What was one time when, as a kid, you got upset because your parents or other adults weren't interested in your ideas?

From **Midlife Manual for Men**:
As a kid your parents pretty much dominate your emotional landscape. They're upset; you're upset. They're happy; you're happy. They're angry, you're scared. As children, basically all we do is respond emotionally to our parents. We're like little emotional slaves to their outsized emotional states.

Son Good Riddance #3: Being emotionally dependent

Just as it takes a while to learn to think for ourselves, so it takes a while to learn to *feel* for ourselves. And it feels *great* to be able to react emotionally the way we naturally want to, not the way our parents set the standard.

How do you remember being chained to your parents' emotions when you were a kid?

From **Midlife Manual for Men**:
We adults come to realize that the "Life 1.0" program that was downloaded and integrated into our own operating system via MomandDad.net contains a few bugs. And at some point along our life path, some of us discover that those bugs have evolved into viruses strong enough to . . . well, cause us to crash sometimes.

Son Good Riddance #4: The things your parents taught you about life that were just plain wrong

Parents usually try to do their best to prepare their kids for the world where they'll be setting those kids loose. But all parents are going to have their share of mistaken ideas and prejudices. And guess what they're going to do with that stuff? That's right—pass it along to the kiddos . . . who then spend the rest of their lives trying to straighten it all out. (Of course, they'll also have *their* own foolish notions, which they likewise will hand down to their kids. And so it goes.)

Let's take an example. If your parents grew up during the Depression, they might have been unwilling to put any money at risk. For them, frugally managing and patiently saving was the right way to handle money. But if you've experimented with investing, you've probably discovered that there's little hope of attaining wealth without taking some financial risks.

Time will uncover many such ways your parents have, in all innocence, misled you.

What things did your parents teach you (either openly or through implication) that you since have found to be unreliable?

From **Midlife Manual for Men**:

As kids we learn from our parents some wrong stuff about ourselves; we then incorporate that stuff into our concept of who we are. When we go out into the world, we jam up in certain areas of our emotional and/or psychological lives. We find we can't do much about those difficult areas of our lives (insofar as we find that trying to change our personality or automatic responses to certain kinds of people, situations, or environments feels like trying to control what our livers or gallbladders do). Finally, we keep plugging away at life anyway, because what other choice do we really have?

Son Good Riddance #5: The things your parents taught you about *you* that were just plain wrong

It's bad enough if our parents give us Bad Messages about something worldly like investing. What if they give us Bad Messages about our identity?

It doesn't take many times for a kid to hear "You'll never amount to anything" before he gets busy not amounting to anything. Or what about the boy who really wants to write novels, and has the talent for it, whose parents tell him that God doesn't want him doing something as frivolous as inventing stories?

Probably when you were a boy you believed the false messages about yourself that your parents taught you because, after all, those messages came from people you looked up to.

Maybe, deep down, you still believe those messages.

What Bad Messages about yourself did your parents teach you?

Today, how can you get out from under the burden Bad Messages have laid on you?

Even though, in our most down moments, it might seem to us that our parents did their best to mess us up, they're still our parents and we still must honor them. We baby boomers famously experienced a "generation gap" with our parents and rebelled against them in our youth. In midlife, though, we can come to a more mature evaluation of them and their legacy to us—loving and honoring them without being blinded to their faults.

This was the experience of . . .

A BIBLICAL SON: JONATHAN

If you've heard of the Old Testament's Jonathan, you probably remember his relationship with David. Preachers have long held up Jonathan as the ideal friend. Yet the Bible tells us Jonathan had another pull on his loyalty: his duty to his father.

Jonathan's story shows us that being a son has never been an easy, uncomplicated proposition. But hey, at least our dads never tried to kill us—twice!

Scene 1 (1 Samuel 13–14): Let's face it, Saul was the sort of dad who easily embarrasses a son. Yes, Saul was king of Israel—a pretty nice gig. But he was also a strange mix of cowardice and aggression. It got him into trouble.

Like the time the Israelites were up against the Philistines. First, Saul proceeded with a religious sacrifice that he, a non-priest, had no right to perform. Second, he brought his army into battle but failed to inspire them with confidence or to initiate any kind of successful action.

Jonathan, meanwhile . . . man, that guy was amazing! Saul's oldest son, with just *one* other guy, routed an enemy outpost, setting up a major Israelite victory. If you've ever seen the old *Sergeant York* movie, starring Gary Cooper, you have some idea of what Jonathan accomplished.

But just when he should have been celebrating, his father did something else stupid.

Check out 1 Samuel 14:24–45.

What do you think of Jonathan's analysis of his father's oath? (See verses 29–30.)

If you were Jonathan in this situation, what feelings would you have about your father?

Was there a time your father made a decision you strongly disagreed with? How did you balance your personal opinion with your duty to honor your father?

Scene 2 (1 Samuel 18–20): Later Jonathan became good friends with David, of stone-in-the-forehead-down-goes-Goliath fame. But Papa Saul—who by this time was becoming more than a little unbalanced in the head—became jealous of David and wanted to kill the young man.

Jonathan managed to patch up the relationship temporarily. And David even married Michal, a daughter of Saul. Yet Jonathan began seeing more and more clearly that Old Dad was more-than-wacko and was determined to get David, even when Saul denied it.

Saul went after David in a place called Ramah.

Read 1 Samuel 20.

How did Jonathan show loyalty to his father?

How did Jonathan show loyalty to David?

How did Saul react to Jonathan?

Does anything in this story remind you of your experience with your own father?

David and Jonathan never met again because David went on the run and Jonathan stayed with his father. But David was there at the battle of Mount Gilboa when Jonathan and Saul were both killed. David's epitaph for them was this: "Saul and Jonathan—in life they were loved and gracious, and in death they were not parted" (2 Samuel 1:23). Jonathan was a loyal (though not blinded) son to the end.

THE BOY INSIDE THE MAN

Jonathan handled being the son of a difficult father fairly well. The rest of us probably did our best to handle whatever challenges were thrown at us in childhood by our parents. And in the process we learned some things about being sons.

From **Midlife Manual for Men**:

Jobs. Briefcases. Neckties. Making sure the margins and borders of the report we've got to turn in Monday morning are all lined up just right. Okay. That's all fine and necessary and good. But in a lot of ways we all understand, it's as boys that we were really the best men we'd ever be, wasn't it?

Son Pure Gold #1: The utter, instinctive joy of being a kid

If you had a Proper Boyhood, you probably get a grin at the corners of your mouth when you think back to a lot of the things you did as a kid. Maybe what comes to your mind first was a one-of-a-kind event, such as the Great Dirt Clod Attack on Mr. Himpelmeier (Meanest Teacher Ever). Or maybe it was something as ordinary as riding bikes with your friends down a country lane to go swimming in a quarry pond on a summer day.

Joy. Boys are good at it. It's sad if we lose the gift of living with joy as we get older. But maybe one way we can start to get it back is to remember what kidhood was like.

What were some of the crazy things you and your kid friends used to do for a good time?

When did you feel the freest, happiest, most yourself as a boy?

Would you like to live with more joy today? If so, how can you get it?

From **Midlife Manual for Men**:

Sometimes we learn life basics via an adult who cares enough to make sure we grasp whatever concept is at hand; sometimes we learn through observing others; sometimes it's just the ol' Elementary School of Hard Knocks. Who knows how or where we learned everything we did? But as boys we learned a lot about life, and every day since then we've built upon that invaluable body of knowledge.

Son Pure Gold #2: Every life lesson we learned as boys

Got a boy of your own? (Or maybe a nephew, or some other little guy in your life?) Does he sometimes make you grit your teeth because it seems he's not listening to you? Oh, he's listening all right.

And *you* were listening when you were a boy. In life's first years, you absorbed an incredible amount of information and principles for living that guide you to this day.

Create your own All I Really Need to Know I Learned in Boyhood list by using the space below to record wise truths you learned before the age of eight.

In what ways do life lessons learned in your boyhood affect your life today? In what ways might you benefit by getting back to those childhood truths?

From **Midlife Manual for Men**:

If you're a kid, you spend a lot of time getting Seriously Harassed, if not outright pounded into the dirt, by that oversized bully-to-end-all-bullies that is General Life. As adults, we sometimes forget how true that is for kids; we tend to think that, like those they're afflicting, the problems of children are small. But as Einstein showed us, everything is relative, and a kid who's gotten himself ostracized from his social group surely suffers no less than the grown man who has, say, gotten himself fired from his job.

Son Pure Gold #3: The emotional wherewithal it took to survive childhood

Some of us had tougher childhoods than others. Some of us were abused and neglected. But even if we didn't have to deal with anything like that, we probably at least had a bully or a teaser to face. Then there were the disappointments and betrayals, such as a friend turning against us or having to move to a city where we didn't know anyone. So much of it seemed like Life-or-Death.

Yet we got through it. And now it takes more to faze us.

What were some of the hardest things you had to face as a boy?

What did you learn from going through these events?

What tough times are you trying to survive right now?

How is the toughness you learned as a boy helping you?

From **Midlife Manual for Men**:

You are always your father's son; you are always your mother's boy. Love your family; hate your family; have mixed feelings about each member of your family—however you feel about them, you realize how *much* of who you are is determined by the family you were born into.

Son Pure Gold #4: The enduring, deeply affective nature of family

If you have a wife and maybe kids, then you probably think of your "family" as you, plus them. But your *other* family—your birth family—still continues to affect you greatly, whether you're in touch with them or not.

How would you describe the health of your relationship with your parents today? With your siblings?

What are some of the best, most enduring values you've received from your birth family?

From **Midlife Manual for Men**:

As men, we have the opportunity to go back and again inhabit the mindset that we had as kids. We *should* learn to at times be that kid again—to sometimes let him come forward and inhabit the body and life that we now call our own. Why not? Our inner little boys are smart. They get it. His instincts, for instance, are impeccable. Someone lies to that kid, he knows it, right away. Something about a situation just doesn't feel right, and all kinds of alarms go off in his head.

COME OUT, COME OUT, INNER CHILD

The poet William Wordsworth famously said, "The Child is the father of the Man." In other words (at least this is what we *think* he meant), the kind of man you are today is dependent on the kind of child you were.

True. And yet that's not the whole story. We also lose a lot of our childhood selves as we grow up. Somewhere in the midst of starting to like kissing girls, learning to put on a necktie, and taking on the role our own fathers used to inhabit, we become Very Serious Grown-Ups.

A shame, in a way. The boys we used to be were pretty fun to be around. And you know what? (*Shh.* This is a secret.) *Those boys are still hiding out inside us.*

That's right. You might not like the pop psych term "inner child" any more than we do, but it's fairly accurate. By using memory and imagination, we, in a sense, can get back in touch with the person we were before we started shaving. And we can learn something from him.

Learn something about being excited about the world.

Learn something about simply having fun.

Learn something about being ready for the unexpected—from ourselves, from other people, and from God.

As you look back at yourself as a boy, what do you like most in what you see?

What lessons could you learn from your younger self about having the heart of a child?

We have another secret to share with you.

God would like to see you open up your heart like you did when you were a boy. He would like you to stop thinking that you always know what you're doing and to start desiring to go along on an adventure with him. He would be eager to speak something new to you if you were to open up to him like that.

Give it a try. What have you got to lose?

A SON'S THINGS TO DO

Check out the "Things to Do" section of chapter 3, on pages 102–104, of *Midlife Manual for Men*. Then enter your responses below.

(1) Letter to father about hurts

If you were to write a letter to your father, telling him about the ways he disappointed or hurt you over the years, what points would you want to include?

Using the points you've listed above, write the letter on a separate sheet of paper. Even if your father is still alive, you won't be mailing it to him. But share it with someone else you trust, such as your wife if you're married. Afterward, answer this . . .

What did writing and discussing the letter do for you?

(2) Letter to father with thanks

If you were to write a second letter to your father, this time telling him that you love him and identifying some of the good things you learned from him, what would it include?

Do either of the following: (1) If your dad is alive, mail the letter to him. (2) If your dad is dead, or if for some other reason it wouldn't be appropriate to mail the letter, share the letter with someone who knew your dad. Later, answer this . . .

What was your father's (or the other person's) reaction to the letter? How did that reaction make you feel?

(3) Earthly father, heavenly Father

In what ways, if any, do you think being your father's son has affected your ideas or experiences related to being a child of God?

(4) Visiting your inner child

Picture yourself as a little boy, maybe in the bedroom of the home where you grew up. Then picture yourself as you are today, sitting down beside that little boy.

What does it feel like to be with him?

Now imagine yourself having a conversation with that boy.

What do you think he would want to say to you?

What do you want to say to him?

(5) Sharing your inner child

If you're married, share with your wife your understanding and discovery of your inner child—that boy you imagined sitting down with. Afterward, answer . . .

What insights did your wife have for you, based on what you told her about the little boy inside you?

Prayer

My heavenly Father, I thank you now for my earthly father and mother. Although they were not perfect, they helped to shape who I am. I'm grateful for all the positive influences they brought into my life.

I thank you, too, for all the good memories of childhood that I have. How fantastic to be a kid! I didn't appreciate all the advantages I had back then, so I thank you for them now.

As for who I am today, I'm wondering . . . what can we do together, you and I, to make me a little less stuffy, a little less serious, a lot more fun? I don't want to act like a fool. But I do want to have the curious, wide-eyed attitude of a child looking at the world. How do you want to make me more open to life—and especially to you?

Heavenly Dad, it's great to be your son!

Amen.

Journey With God Journal

Things I feel God is speaking to me about being as openhearted as a boy:

Notes for My Men's Group

Things I want to be sure to bring up at our third group session:

Notes on the DVD

Things I want to remember from Steve's message in scene 3:

HUSBAND

I (STEVE) PROPOSED to my wife by hiring an airplane to tow a banner reading, "Misty, will you marry me? Steve." It worked! Come to think of it, I should hire that airplane to carry another banner, this time with, "Misty, I love you more than ever! Steve." *

The best thing we men can do for our marriage in midlife is to renew our love for our wife—and to *tell* her of our love.

What do you love about your wife?

(1)

(2)

(3)

(4)

(5)

---

*Not a husband? Then feel free to skip over to chapter 5 of this workbook. But since the husband-wife relationship has so much to reveal about male-female interaction and about love in general, we recommend that you still read chapter 4 of *Midlife Manual for Men*.

From **Midlife Manual for Men**:

> After a while it comes to pass that you and your beautiful wife have been married for twenty or thirty years. And maybe along the way the two of you had children who are now teenagers who like to drive you crazy by wearing black lipstick and/or listening to music that sounds like violence put to a beat. Or maybe your children have left for college, leaving behind an infinite-seeming void. Maybe you and/or your wife have elderly parents you're now taking care of. Maybe your career didn't quite pan out as you assumed it would back when you were nothing but bright ideas and a world of nerve. Maybe your wife's going through menopause. The point is: Things have really changed.

Billy Bob (oddly, not from the South) was married ten years—three years beyond the proverbial "seven-year itch"—when he had an affair with a woman at the factory where he worked. Didn't plan it. Didn't much enjoy it, to be truthful. And didn't continue it for very long. But when it was over, he became overwhelmed one day in church with the idea that he should confess to his wife about what he'd done.

We'll leave it up to you to imagine how Wilma Rae (now, she *was* from the South) reacted to the news. The repercussions from the confession lasted much longer than the affair itself. Billy Bob wasn't always sure the marriage would survive. But in the end a lot of good came out of that confession.

The counseling the couple went through revealed some problems in their marriage that had preceded the affair and that previously they'd only vaguely been aware of. For his part, Billy Bob had been taking his wife for granted, had been acting selfishly, and had been giving his fantasy life full rein. The process they went through began to show him who his wife really was—and he liked her. A lot.

Billy Bob became a much more loving man in the wake of the affair and its revelation. His wife would wake up to find him praying for her on his knees at the foot of their bed. She would find that he'd been thinking about her and had anticipated her smallest needs before they materialized. She received notes, presents, and phone messages from him almost every day.

Today Billy Bob is not only a more loving husband, he's also a more loving father, brother, son, and friend. He became a Real Husband, one who loves and is loved in return. One who knows what that most godly of virtues—love—really is.

That's what we're getting at in chapter 4 of *Midlife Manual for Men* and also in this workbook chapter.

Note: We hope you've been sharing insights from this workbook with your wife all along. Even if not, we encourage you to share *this* chapter. In a few places below we specifically urge you to consult with her. Even better than that would be to work through the entire chapter with your wife sitting right there with you and talking it over with you.

NEWLYWED NO MORE

Movies and TV shows usually glamorize the beginnings of romantic relationships. And yeah, there can be a lot of heat and sparks at that time. It makes for good drama. Remember? But there are some aspects of the early part of a romantic relationship that we're glad to be past by the time we get to the Mellow Middle of Marriage.

From **Midlife Manual for Men**:
> Now we're older, and a whole lot more knowledgeable and secure than we used to be about sex and sexuality and how it relates to our relationship with our wife.

Husband Good Riddance #1: Being basically insane about sex

Let the younger men get all hot and bothered about sex, obsessed with the physical act (or acts) they are performing (or not performing) with their woman (or women). By middle age, we married guys usually have sex put in its place a little better than that.

Of course, it's possible that some of us are like Al Bundy on that crude old TV show *Married . . . With Children*—a middle-aged man sex-obsessed with every woman *except* his wife. Or we may have gotten derailed sexually in some other way. But hopefully sex with your wife is still mutually gratifying and, more important, a warm part of loving her.

How has your attitude toward sex changed since you were, let's say, nineteen?

What role does sex play in your marriage right now?

From **Midlife Manual for Men**:

One of the greatest things about middle age is that it's the time when you finally begin to realize that you really *do* know who you are. You *do* know what makes you tick. You *do* know what you like, what you don't, how you feel, how you don't, what you believe, what you don't. All of it. You have the knowledge it takes to create a marriage so blessedly happy and healthy that it really can be described as a holy matrimony.

Husband Good Riddance #2: All the psychological baggage and lies that stop you from being the greatest husband in the world

It's hard to hide anything from a wife, isn't it? Women have a wonderful—and to men, sometimes unnerving—way of picking up on emotional nuances so slight we didn't even know we had them. A wife can become a mirror to show us who we really are, as opposed to whatever image we've been trying to project.

With our wife's help, and with the passage of time and maybe a little growing wisdom, we can evolve into the sort of person who we like and who our wife is proud to be with. And if that's true, then from here on out marriage can be a truly beautiful thing.

Since being married, how have you come to better understand who you are?

How has this growing self-knowledge made you a better husband?

From ***Midlife Manual for Men***:
Midlife is the time when God deepens and enriches our life experience by showing us that, after all, we don't know our wives anywhere near as well as we think we do. It's a time when God is ready to reveal to us that, just like we're changing, our wives are also changing—which means that between the two of us, there are a lot of new presents on the table, waiting to be unwrapped.

Husband Good Riddance #3: Taking your wife for granted

It's true that in marriage the man and the woman become one. But the danger there is, if someone is that close to you, it's easy to overlook her. You can think, *Well, she's always going to be there, making dinner, taking care of the kids, satisfying me in bed.* We men, with our focus on achieving, are really good at taking our wives for granted.

But our wives deserve more. They deserve to be noticed. They deserve to have their individuality recognized and cultivated so that they can become fulfilled on their own. And they deserve to have us recognize that they're going through their own changes in life, just as we are.

There is no better time than middle age to turn to our wives with consideration, gratitude—and hey, just plain curiosity.

Ask your wife if she feels you have been taking her for granted lately—and tell her you really want an honest response. Summarize her response here:

If you've been taking her for granted, what do you need to change in your behavior?

GETTING TO THE GOOD STUFF

There's more pure enjoyment to be had in marriage—every aspect of it—in midlife than in the years that came before. Let's make the most of this most intimate relationship.

From **Midlife Manual for Men**:

Throughout our marriage, how have we really been spending our time with our wife? Learning about God, that's what. Maybe not purposefully. Maybe not systematically. Maybe not even consciously. But throughout our relationship with our wife, God has always been working behind the scenes, teaching us about love, sacrifice, humility, patience, acceptance. Our marriage is there to teach us just about everything there is to learn in this life that's of real and lasting value.

Husband Pure Gold #1: The invaluable time you've spent with your wife

Sure, you know how many years you've been married (you do, don't you?). But do you know how many *hours* you've been married? Do the math (a calculator may help).

Number of years of marriage celebrated at last anniversary:

_____ x 8760 = _____

Number of months since last anniversary:

_____ x 720 = _____

Add the two totals and you'll get a pretty accurate estimate of the hours you've spent married to your wife—the time you've put into this marriage. So here's our question: What has that time done for you?

We're willing to bet that even if you haven't recognized it, your time with your wife has taught you a lot about God. Since you're a married guy, marriage is helping to mold you into the man God wants you to be.

How has being married to your wife helped you to understand God and his desires for your life?

From ***Midlife Manual for Men***:

What one thing is the key to a happy marriage? Compromise: the ability and willingness to make your own will and your own needs subservient to love. Which is to say, to make your will subservient to God's will.

Husband Pure Gold #2: Understanding the true value of compromise

She wants to visit family on the major holidays; he wants to go someplace with a beach. She wants tickets to plays and concerts; he prefers sporting events. She'd like a bigger house; he'd rather get rid of the clutter and stay put.

Marriage. It's a dance of conflicting interests. And compromise is the key in which the duet is played.

But compromise isn't just about getting through life together with some measure of peace. It's also a way of learning to follow

God better. Mutual submission in marriage (Ephesians 5:21) is a training ground for submitting to God's higher call.

What do you and your wife compromise about?

How good would you say you are at compromising with your wife? Would she agree with your assessment?

How has learning to compromise in marriage made you a better follower of Christ?

From **Midlife Manual for Men**:

That time when you successfully steered the car over onto the shoulder, and then right there on the side of the road changed that flat tire, maybe. Or maybe that time you climbed onto the roof of your house to find out what was going on up there. Or that time you helped that one old woman—or that blind guy, or that kid on the bike, or that cat stuck up in a tree. All of those sorts of things, all of those kinds of times. None of that stuff is ever lost to your wife. She remembers it all.

Husband Pure Gold #3: Being your wife's hero

You might think of being a hero as storming a hill in the teeth of the enemy's artillery fire or as coming between an old woman and the burly dude who wants to relieve her of her jewelry. But your wife likely has a different image of a hero in her mind. Everyday acts of kindness—getting up in the night to comfort a frightened child, going out in a snowstorm to buy medicine when she's sick, seeing that your family's income exceeds expenses every month—can be heroic in her eyes. And guess who stars as the hero in these scenarios: you!

Kind of nice, huh? Puff out that chest, big guy.

Ask your wife if you're her hero. If she says no, ask her to explain why not. If she says yes, ask her to explain why. Summarize her response here:

What could you do differently to be more worthy of playing the role of your wife's hero?

From **Midlife Manual for Men**:

Your life is the medium through which God the Master Artist reveals the full scope and breadth of his creative, infinitely compassionate genius. And he just spent the last chunk of your life painting your life and marriage with his hues, textures, shapes, and perspectives. Middle age finally provides enough distance to view and understand it as the masterful work it is.

Husband Pure Gold #4: Feeling/knowing how deeply God has always been with the two of you

Do you have kids? If so, and especially if your kids are teenagers, we're willing to bet they think you and your wife are boring. The quiet things you enjoy as a couple aren't exciting enough to interest the young. But they fit you and your wife just fine, don't they?

And in this more peaceful, reflective time of life, you can begin to look back and see what God has been doing in your life and in your marriage. You can see his hand shaping your history, forming you into what he wants you to be.

Jesus has been with you and your wife all along. He's with you now. And he's revealing himself more all the time.

Looking back over your marriage, where do you most clearly see Jesus working in your lives?

What do you understand better about God's role in your marriage now than you did when you were younger?

For your wife, for yourself, for the work of God in your lives together, make the most of your marriage. Love your wife more and more and more!

But don't just take our advice. Consider the example of . . .

A BIBLICAL HUSBAND: THE SONG OF SONGS GUY

The story line of the Song of Songs is notoriously hard to follow, like some Russian novels and the *Lord of the Rings* movies. It could be that there are three main characters in Song of Songs: (1) a pretty country girl; (2) a shepherd, whom the girl loves and who loves her back; and (3) King Solomon, who despicably wants to break up the lovers and add the girl to his harem. On the other hand, there may just be two: King Solomon and the country girl he falls in love with and marries. Or maybe it's about a hobbit who tries to destroy a ring; we can't be sure.

But in one sense, it doesn't matter if you can't totally follow the plot. The romance just *pours* out, and that's the main thing.

Try reading the whole book—it won't take you long. If you're using the *New International Version*, you'll see that the speeches are credited to a "Lover" (the guy), a "Beloved" (the girl), and some "Friends" (her girl friends). In chapter 4 we see an example of the extravagant way the two lovers talk to each other.

Read Song of Songs 4:1–15, the Lover's praise of his Beloved.

What's your general impression of how this husband feels about his wife? Think he's impressed?

We realize that metaphors and romantic language have changed over the past three thousand years. (Your wife probably wouldn't know what to say if you compared her hair to a flock of goats or her temples to the halves of a pomegranate.) Even so, women love compliments on their looks.

What praise could you give your wife, in all sincerity, on her beauty?

Read Song of Songs 4:16, the Beloved's response to her Lover.

What did the husband's praises do for his wife? Do you think they had a good night?

What would it do for your wife (and you) if you were to praise her regularly and specifically?

Wait a minute! you might be thinking. *These two are newlyweds. Of course they're all lovey-dovey. So were we at that stage of life. But we've been married for years now—the romance has cooled off.*

Our response: Yeah, but wouldn't you like to get back some of that fire? In midlife, your circumstances (kids growing up, and so on) might be dialing things back to a place where you can focus more on your wife and marriage. Pursuing your wife romantically like in the old days is a great place to start. In the words of Rupert Brooke, "A kiss makes the heart young again and wipes out the years."

Let us conclude with this blessing of Solomon (who, remember, might have been the Song of Songs husband):

> May your fountain be blessed,
> and may you rejoice in the wife of your youth.
> A loving doe, a graceful deer—
> may her breasts satisfy you always,
> may you ever be captivated by her love.
> (Proverbs 5:18–19)

From *Midlife Manual for Men*:

Middle age is all about not having to pretend anymore. Young people need to pretend about who they are because they haven't yet had time to become whoever they're going to be. Well, we *have* had time to become ourselves—and *now* it's time to share the entirety of who we are with the woman who has done so much to form and nurture that very person.

FULL DISCLOSURE

Before we conclude this chapter on love and marriage, there's one more key point we can't leave out. It's about telling the truth between marriage partners.

In chapter 4 of *Midlife Manual for Men* we tell the story of Dan, a guy who's keeping a secret from his wife. Is he a convicted murderer? Does he like to wear women's underclothing? Is he hiding from the mafia? No, he likes to play electric guitar.

Dan's wife doesn't even know he owns an electric guitar. And that's the way he wants to keep it, because he's afraid she would think it means he's holding on to a piece of his rebellious youth. So he only plays after hours at his auto repair shop.

It might seem like an innocent deception. But there are *no* innocent deceptions in marriage. You will do yourself, your wife, and your marriage a favor if you let her know as much about you as you know yourself. (Well, okay, you don't need to tell her what you're thinking about getting her for her birthday.)

Is it possible that disclosing hidden truths about yourself will cause trouble and discomfort in your marriage? Yes. Temporarily, anyway. But it's what it will take for you to make a close relationship even closer. Besides, there's a good chance your wife won't be upset at all about the thing you need to share with her, just as we think Dan's wife might really like his guitar playing. Women *love* it when men disclose.

It's time to stop pretending. Begin getting real now. And begin with your wife.

Do you agree or disagree with the concept that husbands should not keep anything secret from their wives? Explain your reasoning.

If you found out your wife was keeping secrets from you, how would you feel about it?

What harm might keeping secrets from your wife cause your marriage?

What does your wife not know about you that you are now prepared to tell her?

Married Midlife Guy, remember this: Honesty is a key to love. And love is the key to everything.

A HUSBAND'S THINGS TO DO

Check out the "Things to Do" section of chapter 4, on pages 131–133, of *Midlife Manual for Men*. Then enter your responses below.

(1) Five surprising facts

Ask your wife to tell you five things about herself that she thinks you don't know. Record them here:

(1)

(2)

(3)

(4)

(5)

What are five things you don't think your wife knows about you?

(1)

(2)

(3)

(4)

(5)

(2) Disclosure time

What's going on in your life right now that you feel you ought to share with your wife?

(3) Anger reaction

When was the last time you were angry with your wife?

Sometimes we get angry not so much because of what another person did as because of something we're unhappy about with ourselves.

In a situation where you got mad at your wife, was there something inside you that was making you feel uncomfortable or guilty?

What can you do differently the next time you're in a similar situation?

(4) Sex life evaluation

Judge your sex life with your wife in the following categories, with 0 meaning "not at all satisfied" and 10 meaning "perfectly satisfied."

_____ *Frequency*   _____ *Variety*

_____ *Spontaneity*   _____ *Overall enjoyment*

What would you like to try with your wife, sexually, sometime?

Prayer

Dear God, you knew what you were doing when you invented marriage. It's like with Adam and Eve. All that "bone of my bones, flesh of my flesh, becoming one flesh" stuff—that's where it's at. Marriage meets my inner need for intimacy like nothing else in this world ever could.

But God, my marriage is also really hard sometimes. Often, even. I have trouble loving my wife like I should. And I'm sure she feels the same way about me from time to time.

You know all about love. You are love. So I'm asking you to teach me how to love my wife better. Help me to be less selfish, more understanding, and more considerate. Help me grow to become the man you want me to be even as I help her to blossom and bloom into the woman you want her to be.

In Jesus' name, amen.

Journey With God Journal

Things I feel God is speaking to me about being a husband and one who loves well:

Notes for My Men's Group

Things I want to be sure to bring up at our fourth group session:

Notes on the DVD

Things I want to remember from Steve's message in scene 4:

PROVIDER 5

TIME WAS, YOU WERE FREE as a bird. As Dylan sang, you were just "Blowin' in the Wind." Maybe you took to the road like Peter Fonda in *Easy Rider.* A la the Beatles, all you needed was love. Ah, those were the days.

Now you're under it for sure. Probably a wife. (Maybe an ex-wife as well.) Probably a kid or two, or many. A mortgage. Car payments. Contributions to a 529 program, to a 401(k) account, and to Uncle Sam via your 1040 form. It all adds up to a lot of *un*-freedom.

But unless you're a deadbeat dad or have been missing in action as far as your family is concerned, we imagine you're more or less sticking in there and doing your duty as a provider. You're working, paying the bills, putting aside something for a rainy day. As someone once said, "A father carries pictures where his money used to be."

From **Midlife Manual for Men**:

Providing for those whose lives are cleaved to our own is something that we men take very seriously. For sure, if the scientists who spend all their time studying our genes just keep looking, sooner or later they'll find a little cluster on the male genome line that's stamped "Bacon, Bring Home. Must Feed Family."

How do you feel about being a provider for your family? (Check one.)

☐ I resent the burden, frankly.

☐ I consider being a provider my duty and I accept it.

☐ Providing for my family gives me a wonderful sense of satisfaction and fulfillment.

How would you say you're doing as a provider? (Check one.)

☐ My family has all they need and more, and that would continue if I were to die today.

☐ We've got food, shelter, and clothing, but there's much more we could use.

☐ My family is in real need, and I don't know how I'm going to take care of them.

As much as we might enjoy looking back on youthful freedom, fellow midlifer, *these* are the days. We have so many responsibilities because we have so many blessings for which to be thankful. A wife! Children! A nest egg for the future!

But as we said in chapter 1 of *Midlife Manual for Men,* men who hit middle age have an embarrassing tendency to blow money on things they don't really need. Things like Italian sports cars and new wardrobes that don't generationally fit.

Even if we don't fall into that trap/stereotype, in this stage of life we're looking at a growing need to be good providers. At one time buying diapers and baby food seemed expensive. Then there was the orthodontia bill. Now we're looking at college tuition and the mushrooming cost of health insurance and retirement account balances—needing those to be big enough to last as long as we will.

Discouraged? We hope not. That's the last thing we want you to feel. After all, we *know* that God will take care of us as we take care of those who depend upon us.

What we want to do is urge you to be *faithful*. We want to encourage you to hang in there as a provider and in fact to plan for how you can provide even better in the years to come. (Of course, if you do see a good deal on a Boxster, it might be worth a test-drive.)

LIABILITIES

From *Midlife Manual for Men*:

In the final analysis, what we do for money—no matter how much of our physical and emotional time and energy it consumes—remains a pretty narrow trough running through one big field. It can be a deep trough, though. From where we sit, it's just walls on either side of us, the ground below, the strip of sky above, and that's it. That's what we live in. That's what we do every day. That's our work-a-day universe. The great thing is that the older we get, the increasingly shallow our work trough becomes.

Provider Good Riddance #1: Defining yourself by whatever is written on your business card

Most men like to work. Oh sure, we may grumble about our jobs. We may curse our bosses under our breath. We may wish we were more like the guy we know who's pulling down a bigger salary. But still, deep down, we like to work because it makes us feel more like . . . men.

It's easy to see how we can start identifying our worth and our very selves by what we do to earn a living. Yet over time, and especially in midlife, many of us start seeing that the equation MY WORK = ME is too limiting. As we learn more about ourselves, we see that we encompass much more than our marketable skills.

There's more to life than work. There's more to *us* than our work.

As you've gotten older, has your sense of identity become less tied to your job? Why or why not?

What parts of yourself that aren't connected to your moneymaking endeavors do you really like?

From **Midlife Manual for Men**:

The great thing about being middle-aged . . . is that by now you have so much experience working with so many different people that you're in a position to emotionally and intellectually separate yourself from the nonsense. Of course, none of us can ever completely ignore or be immune to the realities of office politics—but after twenty or thirty years, we've reached a point where we understand the nature of office politics and gossip. What finally sinks into us is that all of the "Guess what?" and "Did you hear . . .?" stuff never really amounts to a hill of beans.

Provider Good Riddance #2: The crazy-making gossip and personal politics of the workplace

It doesn't seem to matter: A workplace can be large or small, white collar or blue, filled with churchgoers or rank heathens, yet still it's going to have its politics. You know what we mean—gossip, backbiting, flattery, slander, and all the pitiful rest of it.

When we were younger, we may have plunged into the fray with as much gusto as the next guy (or girl). But as we've gotten older, we started to see through all that. It begins to seem middle schoolish, doesn't it? It's not what the work is really all about, and it's not what life is really all about. We can do without it.

What kinds of gossip and politics have you seen recently at your workplace?

How have you tried to distance yourself from that silliness?

ASSETS

From **Midlife Manual for Men**:
The great thing about being middle-aged is that we *have* worked. Most of us have worked more hours than we'll ever know. It's in our blood now; the work we've done is as much a part of who we are as our shoulder blades and our legs. We *know* from a hard day's night. And that's an eminently comfortable thing to know, too, because life doesn't slow down—even in midlife. Instead, our lives get more complex and dynamic every day. And just as it could be back when we were young, that can still be fairly intimidating for us today.

Provider Pure Gold #1: Knowing that when push comes to shove, you know how to work

A young man starting out in the world of work wonders, *Am I ever going to find a decent job? Where is my place in this great big galaxy of business? Am I going to be accepted, and will I succeed?*

By midlife, though, we've logged more hours working than we can count. We have the satisfaction of knowing what it's like to bring in a paycheck over a period of years, to receive promotions or accolades now and then, maybe even to make a career change and discover that we're capable of doing more than we realized.

Kind of a nice feeling, isn't it?

What has given you confidence about your ability to achieve in the workplace?

How could your self-confidence free you to be more creative as a worker and as a provider in life's second half?

From **Midlife Manual for Men**:

A lot of us in midlife are in a phase where our careers—for myriad reasons—are, or feel, more unsettled than we'd prefer. If that's happening to you, this is a really good time for you to focus on those talents and powers of yours that *belong* to you—that will forever remain with you, no matter what gets merged, downsized, outsourced, or restructured. And one truly valuable life skill you've acquired "simply" by working as long as you have is the nature and value (and, sadly, the rarity) of a true team environment.

Provider Pure Gold #2: The value and joy of true teamwork

You may have a job as a tightrope walker, in which case we hope you're great at working solo. Watch it, now—keep your balance!

But chances are you have a job that requires working in a team. More and more, it seems, that's the way of the business world. Cooperation, more than competition, is the key to success.

And do you know what? By midlife, most of us have gotten over some of our hang-ups and the selfishness that kept us from being team players in our earlier years. We can work in groups—and we like it. The better we get at synergy in the marketplace, the more we enjoy what we do and the more valuable we are to our employers.

86

Teamwork makes the end game of our careers look more enjoyable than ever.

What have you learned about successful teamwork on the job?

What do you like about working on a team?

How might being a team player benefit you as a worker and a provider in the coming years?

From **Midlife Manual for Men**:

The money you've made over your lifetime didn't only keep you alive, it fed, clothed, and housed your family. That fact is so basic we almost forget it—or at least not very often feel the full weight and significance of it.

Provider Pure Gold #3: Knowing that people ate because of you

Maybe you sometimes feel down about your career success. Maybe you're not doing the kind of work you'd most like to do, you're not getting the recognition you feel you deserve, or you haven't received the rewards you'd like to have. Maybe.

But if you're plugging away at your work and are providing for your family's needs, then there's something you can take satisfaction in: You're being faithful at one of our fundamental duties. You're providing. And that's no small thing.

"Good Old Dad, he was always there for us," your kids will say after you're gone.

In all honesty, about what can you congratulate yourself in being a provider?

How does being a provider for your family make you feel?

God knows what you're going through as a provider—the good *and* the bad. He's seen the same drama played out in men's lives throughout history. And in the Bible we can see how he gives blessings with a free hand to men who in turn can share with their loved ones.

A BIBLICAL PROVIDER: ABRAHAM

If we've learned anything about the story of Abraham from sermons or Sunday school, it's probably that he and his wife, Sarah, had to wait until they were senior citizens before birthing the son God had promised to them: Isaac. So what was Abraham doing all those years while they were waiting? In large part, he was gathering the wealth he would pass down to his descendants— once he had descendants, that is.

Abraham didn't read T. Harv Eker's *Secrets of the Millionaire Mind*, Robert Kiyosaki's *Rich Dad's Guide to Investing*, or any of the other how-to-get-rich books that hang out at the heights of today's sales rankings. Yet he managed to amass considerable wealth for the time and place where he lived. Or as he no doubt would have put it, the Lord abundantly blessed him (Genesis 24:35).

Let's take a tour of the financial career of this would-be, finally-was dad.

(1) Abraham started out with seed money. *See Genesis 12:5.* Before he even left Ur (in modern-day Iraq) for the Promised Land, he'd already accumulated possessions and servants. He'd probably received some of this from his father, Terah.

(2) Abraham profited even in a down market. *See Genesis 12:16; 13:2; 20:14, 16.* When market conditions became threatening (e.g., severe famine), Abraham moved his ranching operation to Egypt. There, even though he acted deceptively, he profited and became more wealthy. Later he benefited financially from practicing the same form of deception *again*.

(3) Abraham didn't let business interfere with family. *See Genesis 13:5–9, 14–17.* Abraham and his nephew, Lot, had both become wealthy ranchers, and their herds were beginning to interfere with each other. So to preserve the peace, Abraham generously offered Lot the pick of the land. God then promised the *entire* land to Abraham's descendants.

(4) Abraham didn't let business interfere with his duty to God. *See Genesis 14:22–23.* To give you an idea of how important Abraham had become in the region, he was able to mount a successful military response to a coalition of four invading kings. He gathered loot in the process but insisted on giving a tithe to God's priest.

(5) Abraham understood the importance of a family financial legacy. *See Genesis 15:2–3.* When making out his will, Abraham had penciled in his head servant as his heir, but he boldly told God that he wanted a son to put down as the beneficiary of his estate. God said, "Hang on—it will happen."

(6) Abraham was generous with his time and his goods. *See Genesis 18:1–8.* He was no arrogant CEO or miserly Scrooge with his money. When three "men" (they were actually the Lord

plus two angels, but he didn't know that) arrived at his tent, he served them in the finest spirit of hospitality.

(7) Abraham knew how to negotiate a deal. *See Genesis 18:23–32; 23:3–16.* In a region where haggling over a price with polite toughness was an admired skill, Abraham was a master. You can see it when he negotiated for a burial tomb. You can also see it in the fact that he even haggled with God!

(8) Abraham provided well for the generations to come. *See Genesis 24:10, 35; 30:43.* When it came time for Isaac to marry, Abraham used his wealth to secure the right woman for him. Abraham's grandson Jacob also inherited his entrepreneurial spirit and became rich.

What do you admire most about Abraham's business ability? What do you admire least?

If you were to live past one hundred like Abraham (a possibility), what does that say about your need to build and manage wealth in the years to come?

Do you feel a sense of responsibility to pass on wealth or a thriving business to your children, as Abraham did? Why or why not?

Although Abraham wasn't perfect, his example shows us how followers of God can successfully provide for their loved ones. And it's all because God does the providing first.

LORD PROVIDER

When Abraham was told by God to sacrifice his son—his only son, Isaac, whom he loved—God honored the patriarch's willingness and instead provided a ram for the sacrifice. "So Abraham called that place The Lord Will Provide. And to this day it is said, 'On the mountain of the Lord it will be provided' " (Genesis 22:14).

Lord Provider, or *Yahweh Yireh* in Hebrew, is one of the great biblical names for God. It's a name we should keep in mind as we think of ourselves as providers. We don't have to get all worried about how we're going to take care of our wife and kids, since God is pledged to take care of us.

It was because God owns "the cattle on a thousand hills" (Psalm 50:10) that Abraham could own the cattle on a dozen hills. God is just as rich and as generous today as he was then. (Note to Robert Kiyosaki: God is the original "Rich Dad"!)

"God, who has called you into fellowship with his Son Jesus Christ our Lord, is faithful" (1 Corinthians 1:9). He will be faithful to you.

How much do you worry about being able to provide for your family? (Check one.)

☐ A lot

☐ A little

☐ Not at all

When have you most plainly seen God providing for your or your family's needs?

What could you do to remind yourself of God's provision for you?

91

Do you know why you can be a provider for your dependents? Because God is a provider for you. You can be faithful because God is faithful first.

On the mountain of the Lord it will be provided.

ONWARD AND UPWARD

This chapter may have been making you uncomfortable because right now your career is in some kind of trouble or in the midst of change. If so, it is no big surprise. Our dads and their dads likely had much more stable careers than we do, possibly staying with one company (or even one position) their entire working lives. But the boomer experience is different.

The work world is much more fluid than it was for previous generations. That's good in a way—it opens up far more opportunities. But, let's admit it, it's also *scary*. After years or decades of making a living one way, we can't help wondering if we're prepared to start making a living another way.

If your work situation is stable, you can skip this section of the chapter. But if you *want* to make a career change, or if you think you're going to *need* to make a career change, keep reading.

Check the box indicating the statement that best fits your situation.

- ☐ (1) You want to switch careers and know what you want to do next.

- ☐ (2) You want to change careers but don't know exactly what you'd like to do next.

- ☐ (3) You like your job but fear you're getting squeezed out of it.

Now skip to the numbered section that corresponds to the statement you just checked.

(1) You want to switch careers and know what you want to do next.

How much time have you spent praying about this proposed career change?

What do you feel God is telling you about it?

If you're married, what does your wife think about it?

If you're unsure about receiving the blessing of either God or your wife, we recommend that you be very cautious. Whether or not you decide to go ahead with this switch, remember that God loves you and loves to provide for you—sometimes in ways you least expect.

(2) You want to change careers but don't know exactly what you'd like to do next.

Why do you feel it might be good to change careers now?

What other careers are you interested in?

When does your schedule allow for you to do some serious praying about this serious choice?

We encourage you to educate yourself as much as you can about how to make a career change (finding a new job, starting a business, or whatever) and about the particular careers you might be interested in. A great way to do this is by talking with other midlife men who've been through similar changes.

But more important, you need to be seeking God. We're talking about the kind of prayer where you do *a little talking* to God and *a whole lot of listening* to God. You might pair your praying with some fasting—going without food for a while to sharpen your spiritual senses.

Don't make a move until God clears up your Fuzzy Vision about what he wants you to do with your work life. He will, in his time. He's got your back, friend—even if his time frame might be different from yours!

(3) You like your job but fear you're getting squeezed out of it.

What's happening in your workplace or industry that makes you think your job is in danger?

Which of the following do you think is the best course for you right now? (Check one.)

- ☐ (a) Try to save my job by making myself look valuable to my company.

- ☐ (b) Focus on finding a new job.

- ☐ (c) Both! Try to keep my job while quietly preparing for the possibility of leaving.

If you checked a or c, what fresh ideas or seasoned experience can you use to show higher-ups that you can help to make the company profitable?

If you checked b or c, what steps must you take to find your next job? (Examples: Take an inventory of your skills and interests. Think about whether you want to move, or to change your lifestyle. Learn about different available fields. Start networking in the area[s] of your interest. Get more education. Look into working as a freelancer or starting your own business. Learn job-hunting skills, from résumé writing to interviewing prep. Plan how to manage your money during a job transition.)

If you seriously think you're in danger of losing your job, we urge you to take bold action. Be proactive in either trying to keep that job or else trying to find an equally good (or maybe better!) one. And trust God to take care of you, no matter what happens.

God always honors men who honor him and are faithful in their duty as providers.

A PROVIDER'S THINGS TO DO

Check out the "Things to Do" section of chapter 5, on pages 155–159, of *Midlife Manual for Men*. Then enter your responses on the next page.

Responses:

(1) Reality check

Picture yourself quitting your job tomorrow. What thoughts and feelings come to your heart and mind?

In the list you've made, circle the things you'd categorize as feelings (like "fear" or "relief"). Underline those that represent real issues (such as "couldn't pay mortgage").

Where did your fears come from? Are they appropriate or overblown?

Look at each of the underlined items. How realistic are these? (For example, how soon would you really not be able to pay the mortgage?)

(2) Bad bosses

Make a list of every boss you've ever had whom you seriously disliked. Underneath the name of each, write down what made that person so difficult to work for.

Boss:

Boss:

Boss:

How did you manage to adapt to and survive your jobs working with those bosses?

(3) Dream fulfillment

When you were a kid, what did you want to be when you grew up?

In what ways have you incorporated into your current work the qualities that meant so much to you as a kid?

(4) Ideal future

If you never had to work another day in your life, how would you spend your time?

Thinking about your answer to the above question, what can you do to make your life more like the ideal you have in mind?

Prayer

Dear God, I know that everything belongs to you. You made the universe and you still hold it in your hand. There's no law of scarcity where you're concerned.

I'm grateful to you for the generous way you have provided for me through the years. And I'm grateful to you for how you've provided for my loved ones through me.

As I consider myself in the role of a provider standing in midlife, I pray that you will keep me from greed on the one hand and from fear on the other. Show me what you want me to make of my work life in the career years that remain. Continue to meet my needs and those of my family however those needs may change in the years to come.

Amen.

Journey With God Journal

Things I feel God is speaking to me about being a faithful provider:

Note for My Men's Group

Things I want to be sure to bring up at our fifth group session:

Notes on the DVD

Things I want to remember from Steve's message in scene 5:

FATHER 6

IN THE MOVIE *Father of the Bride,* George Stanley Banks (played by Steve Martin) has trouble sleeping on the night before his daughter's wedding. Images of Annie at different ages flit through his mind. He remembers her smiling as a baby, riding a bike, doing her homework, shooting baskets in the driveway, showing off her cap and gown at graduation.*

At the end of the Memory Lane montage, George goes out to the driveway, where he's heard the sound of a ball bouncing. It's his daughter, the bride-to-be. She can't sleep either and is feeling sad about leaving behind her childhood and her childhood home.

Annie tells her father how hard it was for her to pack up all her memorabilia, things like her yearbooks, her retainer, her magic tricks.

"That's the thing about life," says George—"the surprises, the little things that sneak up on you and grab hold of you. It still happens to me."

Few things are as rewarding for a man as becoming a dad and raising children throughout all their stages and changes. As one psalmist said,

---

*Not a father? In that case, you're welcome to skip chapter 6 and move on to chapter 7. But if you think someday you might be a father, or if you'd like to better understand your own father or another dad in your life, we recommend reading chapter 6 of *Midlife Manual for Men*.

> Sons are a heritage from the Lord,
>> children a reward from him. (Psalm 127:3)

It's also true that few things are as formative for a man as having children.

How has being a dad been a blessing to you?

How has your role as a dad changed over the years?

How has the role of dad changed you?

BAD DAD

Middle-aged dads are afforded a luxury that younger men don't have: We can look back over a longer parenting career and make a more substantial evaluation. Some parts of parenting, to be frank, are nice to leave behind us.

From ***Midlife Manual for Men***:

Raising children is work. And it's hardly the sort of work that sticks to any kind of schedule, is it? Instead, it's the kind of work that cries around the clock, that won't eat spaghetti unless it's cut into uniform lengths, that suddenly *has* to have your help on a school project that should have been started weeks ago, that causes you to pull out all your hair. The scientists are right: Male pattern baldness *is* caused by genetics. It's caused by your kids.

Father Good Riddance #1: The sheer, unending labor of raising young kids

Hearing the cry from the crib again just as you fall back into bed. Developing a backache from bending over the bathtub. Spooning a bite of pureed carrots into a little mouth, only to have it spewed back in your face.

When we're raising little kids, we think, *Will they ever grow up? And even if they do, will I survive it?*

Well, they do grow up. And later we miss all the cute things they did and said when they were young. (Most likely God made little kids so cute just so that parents wouldn't strangle them and the human race wouldn't die out!) But all the body-aging, mind-numbing work of caretaking—*that* we don't miss.

What part of raising young kids do you have no desire to experience again (at least apart from grandkids)?

From **Midlife Manual for Men**:

For many of us, having children who look up to us to fulfill virtually all of their physical, emotional, and intellectual needs can be pretty daunting. But we can't *say* it's daunting; we can't *act* like it's daunting; we can't *admit* that half the time we barely have any more of an idea about what's going on than our kids do. We are men, which means we are the heads of our families, and how would our *not* knowing stuff help anyone? Nobody wants a captain who isn't quite sure how to steer his ship.

Father Good Riddance #2: The burden of always having to be Super, Never-Wrong Dad

Kids have a way of thinking that their parents are experts in everything pertaining to them. And we, as dads, have a way of trying to live up to that expectation. If we don't know it, we'll learn it. If we don't have time to learn it, we'll bluff our way through. It can get pretty funny at times.

As we get older, and as our kids do, we generally become more willing to give up the pretension of being flawless and capable of all things. One cool aspect, though, is that we've learned something along the way.

How did you learn that you didn't need to pretend to know more than you did or pretend to be capable of doing something you couldn't?

From **Midlife Manual for Men**:

Part of being a father is knowing that at times we have let our children down. God knows we have, on occasion, done that. And we know our children know it.

Father Good Riddance #3: The burden of all those times you were something less than the Perfect Dad

By midlife, you should have a fairly good perspective on what kind of a dad you've been. No doubt you made mistakes and regret them. By now, though, you probably understand that you're a mere human, like everybody else, and that you could never hope to be a perfect dad.

But if you still have fathering mistakes weighing on your conscience, there's something you can do about it. You can apologize to your kids. It won't change the past, but it will probably ease your heart . . . and maybe their hearts too.

As you think back on your parenting, what mistakes do you regret the most?

What (if anything) do you still feel you need to apologize for to your children?

While there may be good reasons for you to apologize to your kids, don't overestimate the resentment they might feel toward you. If you ask your kids what kind of a dad they think you've been, chances are good they'll say they most vividly remember the good stuff you did.

GRAD DAD

At the risk of becoming just a wee bit smug, we midlife dads can take satisfaction in what we've accomplished as parents. We've "graduated" to a stage where we've accumulated some wisdom and some appreciation for what we've been through.

From **Midlife Manual for Men**:

When it comes to being a parent, you *did* do your job, didn't you? If you've got a child who now walks, talks, and generally functions like an adult, then your Primary Business has been attended to. Times between you and your child were rough; times were good; times were sweet; times were bitter—but in the end, you did it.

Father Pure Gold #1: Knowing you've done your job

For all the failures you may be keenly aware of in your fathering career, by midlife you can look back upon much that you achieved. Your child is twenty now (or ten or thirty) and is doing all right. Most likely, you kind of like the way he or she has turned out.

Take some time to savor the memories from your years of parenting. Like George Banks in *Father of the Bride,* look back over key moments and vivid memories of your kids. Revel in what God let you achieve and experience.

What are some things you like most about the way your kids have turned out so far?

What gives you the most satisfaction with yourself as you look back over your years of parenting?

From **Midlife Manual for Men**:

Love. Hate. Kindness. Rudeness. Simple, old-fashioned obnoxiousness. It's somehow all part of the same big picture, isn't it? What we find is that everything inside the picture of our lives is painted from the same material: love. And we really understand how true this is when we look back on all the struggles and joys in the years we spent trying our best to create from our children happy, competent, loving adults.

Father Pure Gold #2: Everything you've learned about the nature of love

Meeting your wife taught you one kind of love. Having kids taught you still another.

We love our kids so much that we submit to being awakened at all times of the night, being puked on, patiently teaching elementary subjects, disciplining in ways that uncomfortably remind us of our own fathers, and much more. With kids, we learn the endurance of love, the forgiveness of love, and the pride of love. In the process we learn about God, who *is* love.

What lessons has being a father taught you about love?

How has being a father made you better able to understand God's love?

From **Midlife Manual for Men**:

How many times during the course of raising your kids did you think, *Wow. So this is what my parents struggled with?* And every one of those times you became a little more forgiving toward your own parents, didn't you?

Father Pure Gold #3: Finally understanding exactly what your parents went through

Have you ever had the disconcerting experience of looking in the mirror . . . and seeing your father standing there? Maybe it was the thinning hair, the paunch just north of the belt buckle, or the lines around the eyes.

Well, we've got news for you. Not only are you starting to look like Dad but you're also going through more and more of the experiences Dad went through. And this is good because it helps you understand him and Mom better. And maybe you sympathize with them more.

How has being a father made you more forgiving of your own parents' mistakes?

How has it made you appreciate them more?

Charles Wadsworth said, "By the time a man realizes that maybe his father was right, he usually has a son who thinks he's wrong." Is that where you're at? Well, here's an idea: If your parents are still living, give them a call and thank them for all they've meant to you over the years.

A BIBLICAL FATHER: JACOB

Your father wasn't perfect. You're not a perfect father. In fact, no father is perfect (except the heavenly one, of course), going back in a chain of dads to Adam himself.

Jacob, the father of Israel's twelve tribes, wasn't perfect either. Not a bad dad overall, it would seem. But certainly not perfect. Sound like any father you can think of—like, oh, let's say *you*?

For Jacob, favoritism was a big problem. He just couldn't seem to treat his family members evenhandedly. It started with his wives (he had two official ones and two quasi-ones). Jacob loved Rachel better than the others. And so it was no surprise that he loved her sons better than the sons of his other wives.

The fact that Joseph and Benjamin were born last also had something to do with Jacob's attitude toward them. There's nothing like an older dad for being a doting dad. The drama came in with Rachel's older son, Joseph.

Check out Genesis 37:3–4.

How did Jacob's favoritism sow conflict in the younger generation?

What do you see as your worst flaws as a father? How have they affected your children?

Joseph's ten older brothers didn't only hate him, they acted on their hate. As you know if you've seen *Joseph and the Amazing Technicolor Dreamcoat,* they sold him to slave traders, who in turn took him to Egypt for resale. Meanwhile, to cover their actions, the brothers had to come up with a story their dad would believe.

Check out Genesis 37:31–35.

What price did Jacob pay for the brotherly hatred he'd helped to inspire?

What price have you paid for your own parental mistakes?

Many years later—again according to the *Dreamcoat* musical—the ten older brothers went down to Egypt to negotiate for grain to carry them through a famine. Little did they know that Egypt's vice-president (played by Donny Osmond in the revival production) now was none other than Daddy's Favorite Boy, Joseph, having succeeded in his career beyond their wildest imaginations.

Joseph wanted to see his younger full brother, Benjamin, so he made this a condition for giving the visitors grain. In doing so, he set up another heart pang for his dad, since Benjamin had become Daddy's New Favorite Boy and would now be leaving for Egypt as well.

Check out Genesis 42:33–38.

Do you think Jacob deserved the heart suffering he went through? Why or why not?

How have you sought forgiveness for your fathering errors? How have you sought to correct those errors?

Well, Jacob finally consented to sending Benjamin to Egypt. Donny Osmond revealed his true identity (singing, "I'm a little bit Hebrew, I'm a little bit Egyptian too"). The brothers made up. And then Jacob moved to a nearby retirement facility to spend his final years close to his favored sons.

Despite all the problems caused by Jacob's parenting flaws, the family hung together and, in fact, became rather well-known in later years. (It's not bad having twelve tribes named after you.)

There's a beautiful biblical scene where Jacob, in his old age, talks to his powerful son and extracts a promise from him.

> When the time drew near for Israel to die, he called for his son Joseph and said to him, "If I have found favor in your eyes, put your hand under my thigh and promise that you will show me kindness and faithfulness. Do not bury me in Egypt, but when I rest with my fathers, carry me out of Egypt and bury me where they are buried."
>
> "I will do as you say," he said.
>
> "Swear to me," he said. Then Joseph swore to him, and Israel worshiped as he leaned on the top of his staff. (Genesis 47:29–31)

When Jacob died, his body was accompanied to the burial site by his sons—all twelve of them together.

What consequences of your fathering—good or bad—will you and your children live with in years to come?

From **Midlife Manual for Men**:

One of the things—maybe *the* thing—about raising a child is that it often takes us along a trajectory that begins with our feeling powerful and godlike, and ends with our understanding that the only way to respond to the development and unfolding of a human life is to drop to our knees in humility and reverence to God from whom all such wonders flow.

CUT DOWN TO SIZE

When our wives become pregnant, they can "look forward" to nine months of nausea, backaches, and frequent trips to the bathroom. And that's all before spending an entire night trying to expel a kid through a passage you would never believe he'd fit into.

We men, though, when we learn of the pregnancy, can sit back in comfort and ease and take credit for the new creation. We may not say it, but we're likely thinking, *Hmmm, I did that. What a stud am I!*

The early years of parenthood are exhausting, but even then we get our egos stroked when our kids look up at us adoringly and call, "Daddy!" We can solve their problems, such as shooing the monster from the closet and screwing the training wheels back on the bike. Sometimes our young kids even do what we tell them to do.

We feel nearly all-powerful in the early years. But as time passes we begin to lose our sense of paternal invincibility. Our kids turn out to have wills of their own. They want to become independent. They do things we didn't expect and perhaps didn't want. By the time they're out of the home, we have a boatload of questions and unfulfilled expectations to face in the silence they leave behind.

Fatherhood is a primary means God uses to teach men humility.

How did your children humble you by turning out differently from what you expected?

How did they humble you by developing independence?

How has being a father been good for your spiritual life by making you see the limitations of your control?

As heartwarming as fatherhood can be in moments like the one in *Father of the Bride*, it also forces us to see ourselves in a more realistic way. That puts us right where God wants us: ready to recognize his power and submit to him as our heavenly Dad.

A FATHER'S THINGS TO DO

Check out the "Things to Do" section of chapter 6, on pages 177–179, of *Midlife Manual for Men*. Then enter your responses below.

(1) Your father's qualities

What are some of your father's best qualities?

How are you living out or not living out those same qualities with your children?

What are some of your father's worst qualities?

How are you reflecting or not reflecting those qualities with your own kids?

(2) Apology to children

How have you caused pain for your children lately?

How could you go about apologizing to them for your mistakes?

(3) Overlooked information

Ask each of your children to name five things about himself or herself that he or she believes you're unaware of. Afterward, record those things here:

Child's name:

(1)

(2)

(3)

(4)

(5)

Child's name:
(1)

(2)

(3)

(4)

(5)

Child's name:
(1)

(2)

(3)

(4)

(5)

What would you like your children to know about you that you don't think they already know?

(4) Children's weaknesses

Make a list of what you consider to be weaknesses in each of your children—things such as a tendency to speak disrespectfully. (If you're worried about your kids seeing this list and being hurt by it, just compile the list mentally.)

Child's name:

Child's name:

Child's name:

How are these weaknesses similar to or different from your own?

(5) Letter to child

If you were to write a letter to each of your children telling them how much you love them and what you like about them, what would you want to include?

Use this list to create a letter to each child on separate sheets of paper. Hand-deliver or mail the letters—and enjoy the pleasure it will bring them!

Prayer

Heavenly Father, what a gift it has been to be a father to my children! Thank you for this unequaled opportunity. I ask now that you will meet their needs today and draw them nearer to yourself.

I thank you also for the lessons fatherhood has taught me over the years. In particular, I thank you that fatherhood has chipped away at my prideful ego so I can become more consciously your child, completely dependent on you.

In the years I have left, make me a model of humility and faith so that my children can follow as they go through some of the same kinds of things I've experienced. Amen.

Journey With God Journal

Things I feel God is speaking to me about being a humbled father:

Notes for My Men's Group

Things I want to be sure to bring up at our sixth group session:

Notes on the DVD

Things I want to remember from Steve's message in scene 6:

FACE FORWARD | 7

CONGRATULATIONS TO YOU, boomer midlife friend! You've made it all the way to the last chapter. That means you're no dabbler; you're serious about living the second half of your life with significance.

From **Midlife Manual for Men**:
You're a man whose character has been forged by life, and whose future is going to be shaped by God. All you have to do is open the door to your future, take God's hand, and let him lead you through it.

By now you've learned about the key roles of a midlife man: "he-man," son, husband, provider, and father. More than the roles themselves, however, you've learned about the key *attributes* you've acquired from those roles.

- He-Man: Integrity
- Son: Openheartedness
- Husband: Lovingness
- Provider: Faithfulness
- Father: Humility

As we say in the final chapter of *Midlife Manual for Men,* you don't just *know* about those five qualities. You *possess* them. And the question for you now is, what's next?

What's next is living out your Big Role, the role for which all the other roles have been preparing you, whether you knew it or not. And that Big Role is to be a complete man of God. The formula looks like this:

He-man + Son + Husband + Provider + Father = Man of God

Off the top of your head, what does the term "man of God" mean to you?

In this chapter we'll help you understand better what it means to be a man of God—and especially help you figure out what it means to be the particular man of God he's calling you to be. We don't mean to suggest you aren't already God's man. But we want you to recognize that role more fully and live it out energetically, as a man should.

When and how did you start your relationship with God through believing in his Son, Jesus Christ?

What are some ways God has used you to minister to others?

What would you say is the condition of your relationship with God today?

By "man of God," we're referring to a guy who desires above all else to know God intimately and to do God's will for his life. Being a son, husband, father, and the rest, is great, of course. But we can't forget that Jesus—in one of those startling statements characteristic of him—said that our love for God must be so great that by comparison our love for the others in our lives should look like hate.

"If anyone comes to me and does not hate his father and mother, his wife and children, his brothers and sisters—yes, even his own life—he cannot be my disciple. And anyone who does not carry his cross and follow me cannot be my disciple" (Luke 14:26–27).

Wow! God really wants your highest devotion, doesn't he? And he has every right to. He's your Maker and your Master. More than that, he has big plans for you and he wants you to come along. Never fear: The rewards will far outweigh the costs (Mark 10:29–30).

Seize the adventure. Become, entirely, a man of God!

How do you feel about being used by God, possibly in a very different way, during the second half of life? Excited? Scared? Uncertain?

Let's review each of the key attributes your manly roles have taught you. In particular, let's focus on how those attributes affect your relationship with God. Remember, it all adds up to being a man of God whom he uses for great things.

We'll start with being a "He-Man" with integrity.

121

From **Midlife Manual for Men**:

There's a reason that we, as a culture, associate our men of proven integrity with the image of them (in one way or another) riding off into the sunset. It's because we know that genuine heroes don't care what other men (and—a particular challenge—what *women*) think or say about them. They've learned to entirely disregard that sort of input. They're tuned into something deeper. They're listening to station WGOD.

DOING THE RIGHT THING . . . AGAIN AND AGAIN

If you remember from chapter 2, we looked at how men in our culture like to be seen as He-Men. We may go to ridiculous lengths to portray ourselves that way to others. But the reality is that while we have some considerable strengths and abilities, we're also flawed in ways that the stereotype of a He-Man would never accommodate.

Real men, we learned, have integrity. And integrity is steadfast adherence to God's way of doing things. In other words, we know right from wrong and try to do what's right. Over and over again.

The danger for a man with integrity is that he may start performing not for God's approval but for the approval of other people. Who doesn't like praise from their peers? If it comes, that's all right. But our motivation for living with integrity should be to earn God's "Well done!" not the world's "Atta boy!"

How much does a desire for other people's praise motivate you to accomplish things?

If you were to be totally focused on what God wants you to do, how would you change your words, attitude, and behavior?

From **Midlife Manual for Men**:

God is hoping that by loosening all the old ties upon you—by creating around you open space that you haven't known or existed within for a long time—you will be encouraged to bring forth (and possibly *rediscover*) your original nature: to bring back to the fore of your consciousness the openhearted, happy, spontaneous *boy* nature inside of you.

READY FOR ANYTHING

In chapter 3 we looked at our role as a son and how it has changed from childhood to midlife. We also looked at how *we* have changed. We saw that becoming an adult can needlessly steal the joy and openheartedness we possessed as boys.

The good news is that in midlife we can start getting those back. And do you know what? It will do more than simply make us more fun to be around. It will do more than just help us enjoy life. It will actually open us up to God more.

When we're seriously going about our business, doing our Adult Self thing, we keep our eyes down so to speak. But when we're openhearted and ready for anything, we're looking up, and so God can easily call us to something new.

Sound like a wrongheaded strategy, since we're so often urged to be "mature"? It's not. G. K. Chesterton said, "It may be that [God] has the eternal appetite of infancy; for we have sinned and grown old, and our Father is younger than we."

Open to life and open to God—it's a good thing.

If your twelve-year-old self were to come to the present from the past and observe you for a while, what would that boy see that would make him smile?

How open to God's direction and leading would you say you are?

From **Midlife Manual for Men**:

The something special God has in mind for the second half of our lives (in case we haven't been clear enough on this yet) is for us to become true Men of God. That means living and reflecting as much of *his nature* as possible. And that means being as *loving* as possible; it means being as open to God's love as you can possibly be.

LOVING OUR WIVES AND OURSELVES

Chapter 4 addressed the role of husband. More than anything else we might go through as men, having a wife teaches us about love. With our wife, we open ourselves up to another human being more than with anyone else . . . or at least we should.

What we learn about love from marriage (as well as from other important human relationships) is useful in all of life. Being a man of God means reflecting his nature as much as possible. And reflecting his nature requires that we be as open to his love as possible.

But in midlife there's often a hitch in being open to God's love. We may be pretty good at loving him or loving others, especially loving our wives, but because of all the mistakes and regrets we've accumulated over the years, we may have trouble loving ourselves. And yet that's just what God wants us to do.

Jesus' words imply that we need to learn to love ourselves. After all, being able to love our neighbor as ourselves, as Jesus taught, assumes that we must love ourselves in the first place (Matthew 19:19). And to love ourselves, we have to forgive ourselves for the ways we've messed up over the years.

Midlife is a great season for new starts. It's a time we can confess our sins to God and let ourselves off the hook for what we've done wrong. By putting the bad stuff from life's first half behind us, with the support of our wife and God's offer of forgiveness, we can move clean and clear into the second half.

If you're married, what have you learned about love from your wife?

For what do you need to let yourself off the hook?

From **Midlife Manual for Men**:
God puts a message in the heart of *every* man in middle age about what he should do in the second half of his life; each man simply has to focus in, listen for as long as it takes to hear that message, and then fully trust it once it's discerned.

BEING THERE

As we considered in chapter 5, men feel a responsibility to provide for their families financially. In midlife we may lose our minds temporarily and blow our cash on a Harley or on parachuting lessons. But when we come back to our senses, we see we still have many years ahead in which we'll need to take care of our loved ones. And that calls for faithfulness on our part.

The quality of faithfulness serves us well in our relationship with God. If he asks us to do something new—maybe something that seems so far out of our comfort zone that it's in a different realm altogether—what are we going to do? Well, if we're faithful to him, we'll make sure we understand him right *and then in faith do what he's asking.*

The Lord loves it when we respond to him like Samuel did when he said, "Speak, for your servant is listening" (1 Samuel 3:10), or like Isaiah did when he said, "Here am I. Send me!" (Isaiah 6:8), or like Mary did when she said, "I am the Lord's servant" (Luke 1:38). *That's* being faithful to him.

If you have dependents, what has taking care of them taught you about faithfulness?

Are you ready to say yes to anything God would ask you to do— even if it seems outlandish? If not, what will it take to make you ready?

From **Midlife Manual for Men**:

Real, complete, and sustained humility is about as contrary to human nature as it can be. Unless, of course, you happen to be a man of God. *Then* it's a whole new ball game. Because then you know that in Jesus we find exactly what we need in order to feel righteously humble. Joyfully humble. At once eminently powerful *and* abjectly humble.

GOD FIRST

Fatherhood was the last man role we discussed, in chapter 6. Our position as father never comes to an end, but it does change with time. Kids have a way of going from total dependence to wanting to do things their own way, thank you very much. And we discover along the way that we go from feeling nearly omnipotent to feeling deeply humble.

Humility is another quality that's transferable far beyond a particular masculine role. It's especially appropriate in our relationship with God.

And just to be clear, humility is not wandering around saying, "I'm not worthy, I'm not worthy." It's seeing who we are in comparison to a perfect God. We submit ourselves to God out of our love and gratitude for all he's done for us. Then he can build us up to be whatever he wants us to be.

If you're a father, how far along in the School of Humility has fatherhood taken you? Grade school? Middle school? High school? College? Grad school?

Do you believe that God knows what's best for you? If not, why not?

Wouldn't it be great if we had an example of someone who perfectly summed up humility and all the other virtues of a man of God? Oh, wait a minute . . . we do!

A BIBLICAL MAN FACING FORWARD: JESUS

Son of Man. Son of God. Man of God.

Jesus Christ, more than anyone else either inside or outside the pages of Scripture, shows us what it means to be a man of God at any age. Men, Jesus is our number one model—*of course!*

Let us suggest three reasons why:

- *Jesus did only what his Father told him to do.* "I do exactly what my Father has commanded me" (John 14:31).

- *Jesus said only what his Father told him to say.* "My teaching is not my own. It comes from him who sent me" (John 7:16).

- *Jesus' will never deviated from the Father's will.* "I seek not to please myself but him who sent me" (John 5:30).

Jesus' total commitment to obeying and pleasing his Father included fulfilling even the hardest part of his mission on the earth—the bloody hanging-on-the-cross part. Referring to Jesus' determination to go where he knew he would die, an older version says, "When the time was come that he should be received up, he stedfastly set his face to go to Jerusalem" (Luke 9:51 KJV). Talk about Face Forward!

How does Jesus represent the ideal of manhood to you?

Now here's the thing. Jesus is called "the last Adam" in Scripture for a very good reason (1 Corinthians 15:45). The original man who walked this planet, the first Adam, messed things up for the rest of us by bringing in sin. That's why we have such a hard time being godly men.

Adam was made in God's image. But that image in him, and in all his descendants, has been defaced by sin like graffiti sprayed over an Old Master. By contrast, Jesus as the last Adam reflects the image of God perfectly (2 Corinthians 4:4; Colossians 1:15).

In other words, where Adam got it wrong, Jesus got it right. He shows us what it means to be a one-hundred-percent-godly person. Through following him, we can have the image of God restored in us as a free gift—in part in this life, in full in the life to come.

Check out 1 Corinthians 15:44–49.

What do you think it means to "bear the likeness" of Jesus in this life? In the next life?

How do you want to become more like Jesus?

Not sure you can cut it as a man of God? Oh yes you can! Not through your own willpower, but by Christ's nature given to you through your faith in that committed-to-the-max, image-of-God-restoring, totally awesome Man of God.

From **Midlife Manual for Men**:

Turns out all those preachers, pastors, authors, and calendar makers were right: God *does* have a plan for you! And we're as confident as can be that it is to spend the second half of your life being the man of God for which the first half of your life has so utterly prepared you.

IMITATING CHRIST

Paul said, "Follow my example, as I follow the example of Christ" (1 Corinthians 11:1). We are to be imitators of Christ, that Greatest-of-All Man of God. And that means finding significance in life's second half by doing the Father's will.

God has a plan for you. He has something in mind that only you can accomplish in your unique fashion. What a tragedy if the world were to miss out on what you have to offer! And what a tragedy if you were to miss out on the adventure that following God's will can bring you!

We hope that as you've been moving through this workbook, God has been speaking to you. Maybe you know very well how he's calling you at this point in your life, and your challenge is to have the courage to say yes. Or maybe you still don't know what he's asking, though you'd like to know. In that case you need to keep seeking him.

Either way, don't stop trying to know God better and to know and do his will with more determination than you've given to any other role in your life. That's the calling of a man of God.

What kind of man do you believe God wants you to be in the second half of your life?

What do you believe God wants you to do with the second half of your life?

Now, what are you going to do about it?

A MAN OF GOD'S THINGS TO DO

Check out the "Things to Do" section of chapter 7, on pages 201–209, of *Midlife Manual for Men*. Then enter your responses below.

(1) Prayer

How much time do you put into listening prayer (the kind where you just sit and pay attention to what the Holy Spirit is saying)?

How could you work more listening prayer into your schedule?

(2) Grief for a lost past

What do you miss the most from your youth or young manhood?

Without giving up your fond memories, how could you symbolically say good-bye to what you've lost?

(3) A vacation with your wife

Where could you and your wife go on a fun vacation—just the two of you? How soon will your schedule allow it?

In what ways could you leave behind your Adult Self and let your inner child play on this vacation?

How could you focus on and celebrate your wife during your vacation?

(4) New stuff

What would you like to do that you've never done before and that you know would stretch you?

(5) Your future

If you could have any future you wanted, what would it be like?

If Jesus were present with you in that future, do you think he'd be pleased with it? Why or why not?

(6) Healthier living

What, if anything, would you like to do to become physically healthier (such as eat better, exercise more, or stop smoking)?

What do you think is God's perspective on your physical health practices?

(7) Men's group

If you're not already a part of a group of men around your own age who get together regularly to talk, would you like to be? If yes, what would you most like to get out of the group?

How could you find or start such a group?

Prayer

Father, in the past weeks it's been a privilege to think through what you're calling me to at this stage of life. I may be still learning the specifics, but I'm sure of this: You want me to be a man of God.

You taught me so much in the first half of life. Help me to use that learning to become a greater servant of yours in the second half.

Most of all, I'm asking that you will help me give up my own desires and ambitions at any point where I have become misguided. Help me to gladly take as my own whatever your desires are for the rest of my life. I want to follow along wherever you wish to take me. I'm yours.

At midlife I want to become more like your divine Son. I want to grow up at last to be a man of God.

Amen.

Journey With God Journal

Things I feel God is saying to me about being a man of God:

Notes for My Men's Group

Things I want to be sure to bring up at our seventh group session:

Notes on the DVD

Things I want to remember from Steve's message in scene 7:

ABOUT THE AUTHORS

Stephen Arterburn is founder and chairman of New Life Ministries—the nation's largest faith-based broadcast, counseling, and treatment ministry—and host of the nationally syndicated *New Life Live!* daily radio program heard on more than 180 stations nationwide. A nationally known speaker, he has been featured on *CNN Live* and in the *New York Times, US News & World Report, Rolling Stone,* and many other media outlets.

Steve founded the Women of Faith conferences and is a bestselling author of more than seventy books, including the multimillion selling EVERY MAN'S BATTLE series. He has been nominated for numerous writing awards and won three Gold Medallion awards for writing excellence.

Steve and his family live in Laguna Beach, California. For more information, go to *www.newlife.com.*

John Shore, an experienced writer and editor, is the author of *I'm OK—You're Not: The Message We're Sending Nonbelievers and Why We Should Stop; Penguins, Pain and the Whole Shebang;* and coauthor of *Comma Sense.* He also blogs on *Crosswalk.com.* John and his wife live in San Diego.